For Michi

C000150356

With best wishes for

successfully implementing

KMC 500 Vision

and beyond ...

with both hands.

St. Gallen, 1. December 2015

J. R. Meier

Praise for *The Ambidextrous Organization*

"Jens does a masterful job of defining the 'ambidextrous organization' that can manage the paradoxes of individual competencies and organization capabilities, managing culture as a shared mind-set and personal behavior, and leadership as personal abilities and organization capabilities. This book offers ideas with impact and can be useful in defining organizations as bundles of capabilities more than structure."

–Dave Ulrich, Rensis Likert Professor of Business, University of Michigan; Partner, The RBL Group

"Many company leaders want innovation and profitable growth without changing the way they've operated for years. Other leaders want to rapidly explore new business opportunities without nurturing established practices that ensure financial and operating stability. Jens Maier helps us see – in this insightful and accessible book – how to do both in order to lead effectively."

–Jeff Semenchuk, Chief Innovation Officer, Hyatt Hotels Corporation

"Jens Maier's erudite and entertaining book explains how companies – and individuals – can use 'both hands' to exploit existing competitive advantages and explore new ones. It is a commendable blueprint for tomorrow's corporate world."

–Prof. Eric Cornuel, Director General and CEO, EFMD

"Executives around the world and across industries are challenged to make innovation decisions in an environment often characterized as 'digitization'. This book offers practical insights for executives on how to frame the challenges and to develop solutions for both their organizations and their own leadership careers."

–Zeger Degraeve, Dean, Melbourne Business School

Exploring the New While Exploiting the Now

The Ambidextrous Organization

Jens Maier
Lecturer, University of St. Gallen, Switzerland

First published 2015 by
PALGRAVE MACMILLAN

Palgrave Macmillan in the UK is an imprint of Macmillan Publishers Limited, registered in England, company number 785998, of Houndmills, Basingstoke, Hampshire RG21 6XS.

Palgrave Macmillan in the US is a division of St Martin's Press LLC, 175 Fifth Avenue, New York, NY 10010.

Palgrave Macmillan is the global academic imprint of the above companies and has companies and representatives throughout the world.

Palgrave® and Macmillan® are registered trademarks in the United States, the United Kingdom, Europe and other countries.

ISBN 978–1–137–48812–1

This book is printed on paper suitable for recycling and made from fully managed and sustained forest sources. Logging, pulping and manufacturing processes are expected to conform to the environmental regulations of the country of origin.

A catalogue record for this book is available from the British Library.

A catalog record for this book is available from the Library of Congress.

Typeset by MPS Limited, Chennai, India.

To my parents Gerda and Gerhard Maier

Contents

List of Tables, Figures, and Boxes

Tables

Figures

Boxes

Foreword

Ambidexterity – the use of both hands at first sounds odd to a business professional. At one level it sounds simplistic – of course we are creating the future in our businesses with full energy and with the use of both hands; at another level it sounds quite complicated – can we not have an easier word to describe the fact that in the area of innovation we have to simultaneously improve existing products and processes, whilst exploring new opportunities "beyond" existing products and processes? However, as anyone who has ever been assigned to the running of exploration projects in large organizations can attest to, the challenges of ambidexterity are very real for both organizations and the individual leaders.

For organizations the real danger of being stuck in existing markets is leaving open opportunities to be taken advantage of by new contenders. For individuals, handling both the risk of project success and the risk of having to deal with the enormous personal challenges are the particular political pressures inside organizations.

This book is building a bridge between the ambidextrous organization and the ambidextrous leader. The challenges at both the organizational level and the personal level are clearly identified. In Part II, practical, down to earth approaches are suggested that allow both organizations and individual leaders to be successful at being ambidextrous.

Professor Wolfgang Renz; McGill University

Acknowledgments

This book would not have existed without the insistence of the founder of the FutureWork Forum, Mike Johnson. Mike has observed over many years how my thinking and experience have developed. When I showed him a brief working paper he immediately suggested expanding it into a book. Now, for him, as a prolific author of numerous books, that was easy to say. For me, this book is a first. Mike Johnson's suggestion was quite a challenge. Having spent years as a Business School Scholar, as senior executive in leading global organizations, and as a consultant, my written output has been sparse to put it mildly...

After crossing the Rubicon of deciding to write the book under the great encouragement of first Tamsine O'Riordan and later Stephen Partridge at Palgrave Macmillan, I was pleasantly surprised: It was fun and it was fast. It was fun because I was able to reconcile many happy, successful experiences remembering numerous occasions with great colleagues, clients, and business partners. It was fast, from start to finish in less than nine months. Ok, with a clear structure in place it was straight-forward to connect the various pieces, which I had the chance to test with many executives around the world through both teaching and consulting. However, with speed comes allocation of time: I am very grateful for the encouragement and support from my family because they saw me even less than usual. My particular thanks go to my partner Paat, whose patience and support was much tested, but relentlessly provided.

This book is very much influenced through close collaboration with key colleagues spanning sometimes many years.

From the strategic thinking perspective, the late C.K. Prahalad, Gordon Hewitt, Günter Müller-Stewens, Costas Markides, and Julian Birkinshaw.

From a leadership perspective, Dave Ulrich, the late Sumantra Ghoshal, Heike Bruch, Wolfgang Loos, Gareth Jones, Brent Smith, Thomas Sattelberger, and Hanneke Frese.

From an innovation perspective, Larry Keeley, Roger Moser, Markus Frank, Nader Tavassoli, Christian Garbe, Armin Möhrle, Thomas Meyer, and Heidi Mason.

In the book I have tried to attribute key ideas to the specific individual. However, I do apologize in advance if in the spirit of collaboration I may have missed a clear attribution when it may have been required.

Finally, my special thanks go to Janna Maier who had to go through each chapter in detail, ensuring that her father's writings remain comprehensible and on track.

Introduction – The Case for Ambidextrous Organizations and Ambidextrous Leaders

Ambidexterity – Why is this Important for You and for Your Organization?

Ambidexterity – the use of both hands is not a new concept. The word "ambidextrous" is derived from the Latin roots *ambi-*, meaning "both," and *dexter*, meaning "right" or "favorable." Thus, "ambidextrous" is literally "both right" or "both favorable." Human beings are usually born with two hands. As they progress through life, it quite naturally develops that one hand becomes more dominant. This is recognizable immediately, as when writing or eating, your dominant hand will prevail without you even thinking about it. This type of preferred behavior develops quite early in life. Usually, by the time you reach the end of your teenage years it will be quite fixed. In normal circumstances your preference for behavior kicks in: You put the pen in the dominant hand and you start to write. In the absence of any significant reason for change – for instance, while skiing you break your dominant hand – there is no need to alter that habit. I have yet to meet a person who decides: "Today is the day. From now on I will start to sign my name with the other hand."

The CEO Test

Recently, I was asked by the CEO and the HR Director of a global IT firm, "Leadership? What has this got to do with 'personality?'" In response I gave them a test I learned from my colleague Brent Smith:

> Test step 1: Take a pen and a clean sheet of paper, then sign your name. They looked at me in bewilderment, but still did what I asked them to do. This took seconds; so what?
>
> Now, I explained step 2: Put the pen in your other hand, and sign your name again... Their reaction was a mixture of laughter and embarrassment. I asked: "Are you proud of the result? No? Describe the process: Was it challenging, uncomfortable? This is what ambidexterity feels like – literally, as a first-hand experience.

As the CEO test demonstrated, to use the other hand is usually awkward, uncomfortable, and unfamiliar. However, with a bit of practice it is doable. Imagine the situation of the person who has broken her/his dominant hand in a skiing accident. For the following few weeks that person will have to function using the other hand. Whilst it will be very hard at the beginning, by the time the dominant hand has recovered, I am sure that individual will be quite comfortable using both hands.

What has this got to do with business? And what has this to do with innovation?

Organizations, as well as individuals, have over time developed their dominant hand. Success at using the dominant hand mainly reinforces the successful behavior. This works really well as long as the environment around both the individual and the organization stays stable. However, changes in the environment may force both individuals and organizations to adapt and to, literally, put the pen in the other hand.

In this change, both individuals and organizations can find themselves in the role of the victim (skiing accident) or in the role of the pro-active change agent who purposefully addresses an opportunity overlooked by competitors. Individuals and organizations can therefore look at this issue from both a defensive and a pro-active, attacking stance.

Before we look at the implications at the organizational level, let us first focus on the individual leader and the role of ambidexterity.

The Individual

Having worked with individual leaders for more than 30 years I have observed time and again how these leaders first identify and then use their dominant hand, their own leadership style. This dominant hand will produce results and will lead to advances in their leadership career.

Take, for instance, an example of a young sales person, extraverted and with a high level of conscientiousness. Among the peer group, this person, through visibility and good achievements, may be identified for its first leadership role. Now, with clear goal setting, tight deadlines, and good follow-through, she/he can achieve impressive results. The individual leadership style of "telling" is emerging and the leader can subsequently hone that style. Based on the good performance, it is not a surprise that this person then gets promoted.

At the forefront of the recently promoted individual's mind is the question: "Why did I get promoted?" The answer is clear: Because my leadership style worked. What will this person do in her/his new role? More of the same – it has worked! It is very clear after a few years of leadership experience that the dominant hand is well practiced: Manifested in a style of "telling," clear goal setting, and close follow-through.

The big challenge arises when this person gets exposed to a new leadership context, outside the functional area of expertise. Take for instance the project of collaboration between two organizations or the internal challenge of moving into a general management role, overseeing a number of functional areas. Here the dominant hand of "telling" will clearly not work. In order to succeed here a style of "influencing" may be the recipe for success. The big challenge for the individual leader is: Can she/he use the other hand, influencing? Is the leader able to use both hands?

We have known since Darwin that adaptability matters for the survival of a species. The same is also true for leaders and organizations. Leaders succeed for many different reasons and the leadership literature has tested many hypotheses, only to conclude that it depends. Now, if you ask the question differently – "Why do leaders fail?" – then the answer is much clearer: Lack of adaptability. Exactly, the Darwin conclusion!

So, what does adaptability mean for an individual leader? Adaptability means to understand when and how to use the other hand. So your preference for behavior as an extraverted, highly conscientious individual is to *tell* your subordinates exactly what to do and hold them accountable to clear goals and tight deadlines. However, exactly this preference for behavior may turn out to be completely counter-productive when you find yourself managing a very delicate alliance of business partners whom you need to *influence* to achieve a common goal in an exploration project.

Adaptability means to understand when and how to use the other hand

Adaptability here means to understand that your dominant hand "to tell" will not work and that you have to deliberately "put the pen in the other hand" to "influence."

In your leadership role you also have to remain predictable. That means that the people around you expect authenticity, they want to see the real person. In Chapter 2 we will discuss the T-Model as a framework for the individual challenge of being both adaptable and authentic in more detail.

The Organization

Let us now turn the focus towards ambidexterity in the organizational context. Organizations have to deliver products and services today, to meet the expectations of all stakeholders on a short-term basis. Therefore, a strong operational focus is required to deliver quarter after quarter in a predictable manner. Now, even with such a clear focus on the here and now, organizations also need to prepare for the future, they must innovate.

Innovation matters because it pro-actively offers the opportunity to differentiate and to create new offerings that are unique and wanted by customers. Defensively, innovation is required to respond to changes in the environment, new technologies, and new competitors.

Organizations, like people, have their own history, their own DNA code. Organizations also develop their "dominant" hand. In the organizational context it is called "core competences," following the groundbreaking work of C.K. Prahalad and Gary Hamel (1990).

Innovation

Organizations behave similarly to individuals. They stick to their core competence, their dominant logic, and their dominant hand. Organizations also want to be authentic; hence so much weight is put on values in organizations, emphasizing their corporate DNA code. However, organizations also have to be adaptable to changes in their environment.

In the business literature, ambidexterity is defined as an organization's ability to be:

> aligned and efficient in the management of today's business demands, whilst simultaneously being adaptive to changes in the environment.
> (Duncan, 1976; Tushman & O'Reilly, 1996; Gibson & Birkinshaw, 2004)

This entails using the dominant hand to make incremental changes and using the other hand to address major shifts in the environment. This is then the equivalent to using both hands for the individual, on the one hand to do exploitation and simultaneously with the other hand to do exploration.

Exploitation

This is the word used to describe the ability of an organization to keep the company aligned and efficient in the management of today's business demands. Exploitation refers to the past, the previous investments, the track record of an organization, and the existing customer relationships. The organization is "exploiting" and building on these achievements. Activities usually include continuous improvement, benchmarking, and business process re-engineering.

The outcome of exploitation is maximization of the utility from previous investments, in fact, harvesting. It means that the short-term performance is guaranteed, market share is won or at least maintained, and revenue and profit targets are being met.

The focus on exploitation can secure the short-term survival of an organization, but it does not guarantee its success in the future. In recent years we have seen great companies such as Nokia and Blackberry struggling mightily as they focused on exploitation and continuous improvements at a time when a whole new market with new players was emerging – the smartphone market.

Therefore the biggest challenge for organizations only focusing on exploitation is the capability trap, not being able to respond to environmental changes.

Exploration

This term is used to describe innovation activities beyond the core competencies of the organization: Where new markets and/or new technologies are being explored. Moving beyond the core competencies has the effect of renewing the knowledge base and preparing the organization to discover and shape new markets.

Exploration sounds very exciting and lucrative at first sight. However, examples of companies such as Eastman Kodak or Xerox, or even Motorola, demonstrate the dangers of exploration. It is very easy to fall into the trap of a potentially endless cycle of search and unrewarding change, without maximizing the potential of all the exploration efforts translated into groundbreaking products or services.

As early as 1993 a simple rule was determined for organizations: Engage in enough exploitation to ensure the organization's current viability and enough exploration to ensure future viability (Levinthal & March, 1993).

To provide an example of organizational ambidexterity and to illustrate the difference between exploitation and exploration, let us use the example of one of the most admired organizations of our times, Apple.

In the Apple product line in 2014 you would have found, for instance, the MacBook Air. Somehow you can trace the roots of today's MacBook Air to the Apple Lisa way back in 1983. Of course the functionalities have changed; the size and power as well. However, as an individual user you could have moved with the Apple generations to support you in your individual work in both private and professional applications. This is a good example of how Apple was able to use "exploitation" as a powerful innovation tool to stay aligned with the changing times and their competitors.

Now, with the advent of new products and services around the iPod, iPhone and iPad exploitation alone cannot be the explanation. These new products and services are the results of "exploration" activities. Each of these three much admired products and the associated services created a new competitive space.

The iPod, for instance, in conjunction with iTunes became a groundbreaking new device for music lovers who wanted individual song titles – legally. The iPhone became the epitome of a new category, the "smartphone," and the iPad created the category today known as tablets. Whilst with the launch of each of these products and associated services new categories and new competitive spaces were established, the journey did not stop there. Regularly each of these products was updated and fine-tuned. So when, in the summer of 2014, the Apple user eagerly awaited the launch of the iPhone 6, the implication was that this model represented the sixth generation of the iPhone. Now, how were these new generations created: Yes, through exploitation, not exploration!

With its track record over the years Apple has demonstrated good performance in ambidexterity, of purposefully linking and aligning both exploration and exploitation processes. Exploration gives you the opportunity to create a new competitive space. However, this is not enough. Within that new competitive space exploitation activities have to follow in order to protect the position in this newly attractive space.

Implications for this Book

This book works at two levels:

1) **At the level of the individual leader.** How can you excel at the ambidexterity challenge and make a significant contribution to the organization and your own career – in possible roles as architect, project leader, or implementer?
2) **At the organizational level.** How can a company create the appropriate levels of capabilities to take advantage of the huge opportunities presented by being an ambidextrous organization? How can the right organizational architecture be created?

Both individual leaders and organizations need to be authentic and adaptable. This means they have to embrace the notion of "innovation." Innovation comes on scales ranging from continuous improvement based on benchmarking, to fundamentally rethinking the business. We all remember the famous story of how Nokia turned itself from a manufacturer of rubber boots into the world's top mobile phone manufacturer. You do not achieve that through continuous improvement or benchmarking!

From Ambidexterity to Dealing with Convergence – The Drivers

In a 2013 survey of the most innovative organizations, Boston Consulting Group (BCG) identified some eight car companies among the top 20 most admired organizations. The headline was: "The car as mobile data center."

Now, most of us admire car companies for being so innovative around the ever-expanding product range. For example BMW, in the past known for their 3-Series, 5-Series, and 7-Series, now produce the full range – 1-Series to 8-Series. Not just the normal four door versions either, but also the coupé, SUV, and open-top versions within each series. One can imagine how busy the research & development (R&D) departments must have been and will have to continue to be in order to maintain the freshness of all the models introduced.

Looking at the performance in terms of model range, BMW and most of its competitors have achieved a lot to merit being included in the list of most admired companies for innovation. However, model range innovation was not cited by BCG as the key reason for being most innovative, but "the car as a mobile data center."

The concept of convergence must be understood in order to unravel the link between cars and data centers. Data centers are associated with server farms, IT organizations, maybe telecommunications companies, perhaps Google or Amazon. As much as individuals and organizations like to feel comfortable in their normal habitat, there are outside forces that disturb that comfort. These are changes taking place beyond the control of any individual or any organization.

One of the key outcomes has been the convergence of industries, which had previously been quite separate: For instance, the car industry and IT organizations. In 2014 Google showcased their driverless car concept. As an organization Google has been greatly associated with the IT industry. What is Google doing in the car industry? This is an example of convergence. However, convergence is not only taking place in the car industry, it is in fact prevalent across many industries.

It is best to explain with a personal story. In the Autumn of 2012 I was working with the top management teams of companies from the following very diverse industries:

- Telecommunication.
- Pharmaceuticals.

- Washing powder.
- Postal services.
- Biotechnology.
- Financial services.

When discussing opportunities for 2017/18, what struck me was that the executives of these companies talked about the same thing: Access to the individual household – and what extra products or services they could offer.

However, what all these discussions had in common was that the opportunities were all outside of each company's own individual core competencies. Each of these organizations had to think "beyond" their own industry boundaries to assemble the necessary capabilities for the opportunities so quickly identified.

The oil company BP made a virtue of addressing these opportunities a few years back when they introduced the tag-line "BP-Beyond Petroleum" as a main part of their global advertising campaigns.

In recent years, in many organizations, units have been formed to innovate "beyond." In pharmaceuticals it is called "beyond the pill." These are examples of how organizations respond to convergence and try to be ambidextrous: In pharmaceuticals, for instance, exploitation is being taken care of in the normal R&D departments and through the well-established R&D processes. Then, parallel units address the exploration opportunities around innovating beyond the pill.

As Individuals and Companies Address the Issue of Ambidexterity

Mega trends, such as aging population, drive convergence between industries. Older people not only need more and more medicine, they also have to take it. In order to be effective, it is important to understand compliance: Has the patient actually taken the medicine? Here it is innovation beyond the pill – the information on whether the pill has been taken is important. Who has the capabilities? It is a combination of capabilities traditionally associated with pharmaceuticals, diagnostics (has the person taken the pill?), and telecoms (information flow). The implications for all three industries are as follows: How do companies polish the existing business (exploitation – develop better pills) and at the same time take advantage of "shaping game" opportunities (exploration – innovation beyond the pill)?

Linking Leadership Development to Corporate Development

This book aims at building the bridge between the need to be successful at ambidexterity at both the individual and the organizational level. The two organizational processes that therefore need to be connected are:

• Corporate development; and
• Individual development (leadership development).

Many organizations have ambidexterity already on the strategic agenda. For those organizations it is then the challenge of how they can move from diagnosis into action.

It requires development at two levels:

1) Individual – can we build the individual's competencies?
2) Organizational – can we build the right capabilities (e.g. robust processes) to handle ambidexterity?

Key Message of this Book

Convergence between markets and technologies happens around us. Leaders have to steer their organizations through this unchartered territory. Traditional management approaches will not work. Both leaders and their organizations have to be geared

Both leaders and their organizations have to be geared towards ambidexterity

towards ambidexterity: With one hand exploiting the current business and the other simultaneously exploring new opportunities that arise through converging technologies and markets. This has implications at two levels:

1) The organization – how can the whole organization embrace the simultaneous processes of exploitation and exploration?
2) The individual leader – how can you personally balance the different demands of both exploiting and exploring?

Structure of this Book

This book is divided into two parts. Part I identifies the challenges around building successful ambidextrous organizations and Part II identifies solutions to building ambidextrous organizations.

In Part I the key challenges will be identified from a number of different angles:

Chapter 1 looks from the organizational perspective at strategic challenges and the need for being ambidextrous.

Chapter 2 looks at the challenges through the eyes of individual leaders inside the organization.

Chapter 3 lays out the challenges around internal processes for exploitation projects and exploration projects.

Chapter 4 discusses the mindset challenges both at the organizational level and at the individual level.

In Part II possible solutions will be discussed from a number of different angles:

Chapter 5 looks at linking two aspects of development: Corporate and individual development.

Chapter 6 looks at the solutions provided by external scouting activities.

Chapter 7 lays out the role of purposeful engineering in creating appropriate partnerships.

Chapter 8 discusses approaches to managing risk. How to de-risk the exposure inherent in convergence for both the organization and the individuals?

Part I

Challenges

Introduction to Part I

Why is this Important for You and Your Organization?

In Part I we will investigate the challenges around ambidexterity at both the individual and the organizational level. Therefore, in four separate chapters we will discuss:

1) The strategic challenges; challenges at the organizational level.
2) The leadership challenges; the focus being on the individual leader.
3) The process challenges; these are challenges at the organizational level.
4) The mindset challenges; the influence of the "dominant logic" on both the organization and the individual.

At the end of Part I we will have built the foundation upon which we can then discuss possible solutions in Part II.

In this introduction, we will first highlight the generic challenges for individuals in organizations by discussing the concept of the roles of managers and leaders.

Then we will focus on the challenges for organizations based on discussions with global learning and development (L&D) experts from large organizations and leading business schools.

The Individual Perspective: The Roles of Manager and Leader

Organizations have their strategic plans, their processes for innovation. These have to be implemented by individuals, real people. Implementation of a plan cannot be achieved with a spreadsheet, it requires real people who drive the plans and the ideas forward.

These real people will have their own personal agendas and goals. The intersection between these two perspectives is clear. Organizations can provide certain formal "roles," like Head of Corporate Development, Head of Research, and so on. These formal roles go along with formal descriptions of the role, including the responsibilities entailed. Individuals have the option to apply for these formal roles.

Now, having a formal role provides clarity for both the organization and the individual. However, just having a formal role and an individual in that role will not lead to any action by itself. It is the actual interpretation of that role that leads to action.

In this section two concepts around roles of individuals are being presented, the formal role as well as the project/change role. The objective is first to provide two different perspectives from which an individual can look at the ambidextrous business, and then to create the clarity to enable them to see clearly.

We will first look at how this fits in with the formal day-to-day role of manager and leader, and then we will examine the view from the project/change perspective.

The formal perspective

As Head of Corporate Development or as Head of Research, you will have a clear job description around your role and responsibilities. In addition, you will have agreed clear goals and deliverables with your boss for the next 12 months.

TABLE I.1   Roles of Managers and Leaders

Leader	Manager
• Create	• Implement
• Innovate for entire organization	• Administer within a sub-system
• Develop	• Maintain
• Think long term	• Think short term
• Ask what and why	• Ask how and when
• Challenge the status quo	• Accept the status quo
• Create vision and meaning	• Act within established culture
• Induce change in people	• Induce compliance in people
• Do the right things	• Do things right

Source: Bennis (1989); Conger/Kanungo (1998).

Now, how these agreements are interpreted is a question of choice for the individual. A useful differentiation is the idea of spelling out the potential differences between the roles of "managers" and "leaders."

The following messages are important here:

• These are not two different people; these are two different roles.
• This is not dependent on hierarchy; the leadership literature is quite clear: We need leadership at all levels.

How is this related to ambidexterity?

For exploitation projects, such as continuous improvement, you can achieve a lot if you take the perspective of the role of "manager." For exploration projects however, it is imperative you take the "leader" perspective. In exploration projects you have to challenge the status quo.

Peter Drucker put it so elegantly:

• Managers do things right.
• Leaders do the right things.

As an ambidextrous leader you have to know when and how to use one hand (manager/exploitation) and when and how to use the other (leader/exploration).

The project perspective

Formal roles apply for the running of the "normal" business. Innovation and change however, are much more influenced by a project mindset. This means that the organization has identified a specific challenge that the normal organizational structure is not able to handle. In terms of innovation, the trigger can be either from a pro-active opportunity or through a defensive, reactive response to protect existing territory.

In both situations requiring a project mindset, you can find yourself in potentially three different roles:

- Architect.
- Project leader.
- Implementer.

Architect

In the role of the architect you are responsible for creating the whole architecture around innovation for the organization. This implies you have to assign roles and responsibilities for both exploitation and exploration projects. Most importantly, you are also responsible for the design of the different processes for exploitation and exploration projects.

The key elements of the architect's role are:

- Strategizing – to purposefully identify opportunities and possible threats.
- Unfreezing – generating a sense of urgency for the organization to change.
- Creating a leadership coalition.
- Building an alliance of key stakeholders to address the challenge.
- Focusing on goals, values, and business results.

Project Leader

You may find yourself in the role of change implementer. In this role you will be formally assigned leader of an innovation/change project. Here you are in a project mindset; you are the translator of the architect's vision and need to see all the implications of that vision at the division and/or department level.

The project leader's role entails:

- Coordinating the internal resources required for success.
- Delivering on expectations.
- Overcoming resistance and creating the necessary buy-in from various constituencies.
- Focusing on moving the organization.

Implementer

You may find yourself at the receiving end of an innovation/change initiative. The architect and project leader have already delivered on their responsibilities. This is no longer the time to question, or to re-open, old discussions. The simple task is to get it done locally.

Therefore, this role is about institutionalizing the new way of doing things. At the local level, the implementer role is about:

- Winning hearts and minds for innovation/change.
- Identifying and communicating the personal benefits to the local stakeholders.
- Refreezing – anchoring the innovation/change process into the "new normal" of day-to-day business locally.

The Organizational Perspective

Many organizations seem to face the challenges of ambidexterity. Therefore, it is not a surprise that this topic is also high on the agenda of the European Foundation of Management Development (EFMD).

The EFMD provides a forum for leading business schools and organizations to address the common professional challenges in management development.

A recent EFMD conference at the University of St. Gallen addressed the topic of ambidexterity,[1] attracting participants from business schools, corporate partners, and educational suppliers from four continents. The focus of the discussion was very much on how to best link a strategic issue, building an ambidextrous organization, to the issue of developing individual leaders. The participants were asked:

> What do you observe in your organization/client organizations? On a spectrum:
>
> 1) Topic ignored.
> 2) Background noise – one of those trends.
> 3) Individual ambassadors, like Head of Strategy, Head of Learning and Development.
> 4) Top team agenda.
> 5) Call to action: top team – strategy – learning and development.

The most frequent score was 3, "individual ambassadors." Here we are talking about people in functions such as business development, Head of Strategy and Head of Learning and Development. In these roles individuals have to look to the future with a time horizon well beyond the current budget year. This result was confirmation of observations made during client discussions over the previous few months.

The next most frequent score was 2, the category of background noise, one of those trends. This is the perspective of "interesting, but so what." This could be seen as one of those management fads, of which we have seen many come and go in previous years. However, organizations and

---

1. EFMD Executive Development Conference – (EI)2 Exploiting/improving AND Exploring/innovating (https://www.efmd.org/index.php/events/event/ 193-2014-efmd-executive-development-conference).

business schools need to be aware of these trends and should have a position on how best to embed them into normal activities.

Some 10 per cent of the participants reported that, indeed, ambidexterity is already on the agenda of the top team in the organization. However, the lowest score was reported for the call to action option with the strong alignment between the top team, strategy, and leadership development.

What are the conclusions from this (non-representative) survey?

- The level of awareness for the topic of ambidexterity is high among the potential opinion leaders such as head of strategy and head of L&D.
- Apart from a few exceptions, these potential opinion leaders have not yet created the momentum to address the challenges of ambidexterity.

When probing deeper into the reasons for the lack of momentum, some of the frequently quoted observations are:

- "In the organization it is expected to be innovative, but play by the rules."
- "Incentive structures do not support innovation."
- "Lack of communication: Strategy, organizational development, learning and development, quality management do not talk with each other."
- "If it is not in the strategy, it is out."
- "Lack of senior sponsorship."
- "No tolerance of risk and failure."

Now, these observations in organizations are not new. Indeed, I have seen exactly the same points being made about innovation in numerous studies I have personally conducted in the last 25 years and many other studies have also shown similar results.

How is it that the same organizational issues are being quoted time and again? How come we make the same observations in organizations even after all the technological and organizational progress over the last 25 years? More importantly, what can you do about changing that?

Implications for Part I

In Part I we will address the challenges around ambidexterity in more detail to get under the surface of the issues. The challenges will be addressed both from a personal and an organizational perspective.

chapter 1

Strategic Challenges

Why is this Important for You and for Your Organization?

In your role as a leader you are expected to understand, challenge, and develop the strategic agenda of your organization. That means, on the one hand you are expected to exploit and on the other hand to explore on behalf of the organization. This chapter aims to provide the conceptual underpinnings for Ambidexterity from an organizational perspective. At the organizational level, a shared understanding of the strategic challenges and opportunities is required to take the appropriate actions. We will look at the theoretical frameworks that we need to understand to discuss ambidexterity in an organizational context.

Two Examples

Example 1: Nespresso

Nespresso has been around for more than 20 years but the story of its development provides an early example of ambidexterity. In the 1990s, Nestlé already had a longstanding instant coffee brand – Nescafé. However, in parallel – and with the other hand – Nespresso was launched. Today, Nespresso has an increasing following around the world, apparently delivering a great customer experience. In fact, in my executive teaching on innovation I regularly ask the question:

- Who is privately a Nespresso customer?
  - 90 per cent of hands go up.
- Is anyone *not* happy with the Nespresso experience?
  - No hands go up, with very few exceptions.

Let us have a quick look at why Nespresso is an example for ambidexterity of the Nestlé organization. Core elements are:

- System: Innovation beyond coffee to package both coffee *and* machine; Nestlé had to build the partnerships with the machine manufacturers.
- Own shops: Created own Nespresso Shops, therefore bypassing the traditional retailers used for Nescafé.
- Customers consist of a "segment of one": Consumers can become a member of the Nespresso Club, where they and their preferences are known individually instead of being an anonymous member of a "market segment."
- Customer experience: Nespresso demonstrates the strategic move from transaction (selling a cup of coffee) to an individual relationship with customers.

In any case, Nespresso is very successful today in taking the transactional consumption of a cup of coffee at home or in the office into the sphere of a meaningful customer experience, in fact, creating a true customer relationship.

The success of Nespresso has meanwhile created a number of followers, including Senseo, a joint venture between Philips, the appliance manufacturer and Douwe Egberts, the coffee maker. Through the competition between Nespresso and Senseo, all of a sudden Philips and Nestlé are competing against each other. Now, from a strategy perspective, it is very interesting to observe that the main drivers – Nestlé and Philips – are usually competing in completely different industries. Both Philips and

Nestlé are examples of ambidextrous organizations. However, this also demonstrates that ambidextrous organizations may have to deal with new competitors coming from different industries.

Example 2: Family business

Here is an example from a business based in Thailand, now run as a family business. The Managing Director explains:

> My parents started this company to do pharmaceutical manufacturing. They focused on drugs initially, beauty products later. Today we are a contract producer for global companies in the pharmaceutical area. In the last three years we launched three new plants.

As the Managing Director is charging ahead, they have not lost the tradition of using traditional Thai plants and medicines. So today they simultaneously innovate in healthy coffee, cosmetics, and prescription drugs. When I told him that he and his organization would be a key example of an ambidextrous organization, and an ambidextrous leader, he pointed out his parents had done the same – this is just how he had grown up, pushing simultaneously the existing business and exploring new opportunities. Ok, the tradition of the Asian family business may be an explanation for the success. However, in his busy office among all the project ideas and samples I could also see a document displayed on the wall: His PhD degree from a prestigious university, where he recently completed their entrepreneurship program – maybe a dose of both family tradition and business school education may be the secret?

Theory: The Ambidextrous Organization

Duncan introduced ambidexterity, the ability to use both hands to the management literature back in 1976. One hand remains aligned and efficient in dealing with today's business demands (exploitation) whilst the other hand stays adaptive to changes in the business environment (exploration).

For many years the concept of ambidexterity was deeply anchored in the strategy part of the management literature. In particular, March (1991) and Tushman and O'Reilly (1996) pushed the boundaries both academically as well as for practitioners, focusing on ambidextrous *organizations*.

More recently, ambidexterity was also embraced by the literature focusing on "leadership." Raisch and Birkinshaw (2008) can be cited as the authors shaping that agenda. Their focus was very much on how *individual leaders* can foster ambidexterity in their organizations.

Numerous academic studies have been conducted at both the organizational and the leadership levels, a good summary can be found in Simsek (2009).

Summary of key findings in ambidexterity research

The following section attempts to summarize key findings from hundreds of studies to provide a general picture. Therefore, the focus is on generalization rather than on the exceptions.

Key finding 1: Ambidextrous organizations are more successful. (March, 1991; Tushman and O'Reilly, 1996; Raisch & Birkinshaw, 2008; Simsek 2009.)

That means that organizations able to reconcile both exploitation and exploration simultaneously outperform organizations, which are one-handed. Measure: ROI, growth, and shareholder value.

Key Finding 2: Contextual ambidexterity delivers better performance than structural ambidexterity (Gibson & Birkinshaw 2004).

Structural ambidexterity

Some organizations structurally separate exploitation from exploration by creating units outside the normal in-house "R&D" structures. This approach was apparently taken when Nestlé launched Nespresso.

Expected benefits include:

- Exploration projects can be set up in an environment which is distant to the traditional exploitation culture, undisturbed with its own processes and measures for success.
- Allows for recruitment of talent from outside.

Potential pitfalls include:

- Re-integration: Challenge to integrate the finished innovation project into mainstream activities; cultural resistance around "not invented here."
- Consolidation takes place high up in the corporate hierarchy – leaving room for corporate politics instead of focusing on project merit.

Contextual ambidexterity

Organizations pursuing this approach trust that individual executives in their normal function know how to operate in both exploitation and exploration mode. This is the approach taken by the Thai organization in the second example at the beginning of this chapter.

Expected benefits include:

- Empowerment: Responsibility rests with individual executives to reconcile the roles of both manager (exploitation) and leader (exploration).
- Link to research demonstrating that leadership at all levels leads to outperformance at the organizational level.

Potential pitfalls include:

- Under pressure, can executives maintain the balance between exploitation and exploration?
- Can they remain consistent in applying different processes and reward systems?
- Can executives deal with these tensions at the individual level?

Implications

The finding that contextual ambidexterity is leading to better outcomes than structural ambidexterity is also related to a consistent finding in the leadership literature, namely that leadership at all levels leads to better organizational performance. However, that means that executives are really challenged to develop the competence to use both hands and become ambidextrous leaders. The individual leader is the key – she/he needs to be able to switch behavior according to whether they are dealing with exploitation or exploration projects

executives are really challenged to develop the competence to use both hands and become ambidextrous leaders

Strategy Concepts in Context

To put this in its historic context: In the late 1980s and early 1990s, there were early signs of convergence, for instance the well documented case of American Airlines who created more profits from their reservation system SABRE than from flying passenger aircraft, their core business. There was a well-received article in the *Harvard Business Review* explaining the power of marketing and information technology, documenting the rise of the Staples Retail concept in the US.

I launched an MBA elective course called "Marketing & IT" in 1988 at Warwick Business School. In this course we were investigating the use of IT to support traditional marketing functions, such as sales, through the newly available databases based on the postal code system in the UK. However, we were additionally investigating how IT could also be the source for creating new markets, inspired by the American Airlines example.

This was all well before the times of Google, Facebook, and Amazon. By the way, in 1988 there was no Internet and the general public had no access to or awareness of the concept of a "mobile phone."

Now, this was all being done at a time when the main strategy concept consisted of Porter's Five Forces. Generations of MBA students have, since 1980, studied the Porter model, which tries to unravel the attractiveness of competing in a given industry. It very comprehensively calls for an analysis of the power of:

- Customers; number of potential customers, their buying power.
- Suppliers; number of suppliers, their level of uniqueness.
- New entrants; understanding the potentially high or low levels to enter an existing market.
- Substitutes; the potential of an unrelated product or service to offer similar utility.

Finally, the Porter model then addresses the level of rivalry within an industry.

It is proof of the robustness of this model that even more than 30 years after its inception it is still governing the thinking of leaders around the world. Therefore, it is worth putting the Porter model in the context of the ambidextrous organization. The starting point of Porter's model is the "industry." This means you take it as given that you are in pharmaceuticals, telecoms, or insurance. Yes, there may be new entries or there may be substitutes but, in the end, it is the "industry" that matters. In our discussion around ambidexterity, this approach is very much in line with one-handed "exploitation." Simply put, by taking the industry as given, any strategies emerging from the Porter model would point to strategy as "playing the existing game better."

The analogy can be seen in sports. If you play soccer you have to accept the rules: The game lasts 90 minutes, there are 11 players on each side, the pitch has certain measurements. If you want to play soccer, you have to conform to the rules of the game, such as penalty and offside.

If you accept the rules and you agree to compete in playing "soccer," the only way to differentiate yourself from other players is to train harder. The translation into business is that you must get better at market research, segmentation, and targeting to win market share.

The Porter model has proven to be very robust in providing insights into competing in existing industries, it is very helpful in one aspect of ambidexterity, namely, exploitation.

So, what are the models that help us understand the other hand, exploration?

I have already addressed the power of convergence, the emergence of new markets, new industries such as the car as a mobile data center, the smartphone, and the tablet market. In exploration there is often no reference point by way of an industry or a market. The Porter model, which starts with a given industry, is of limited use here.

Shaping: Influencing; stake in the ground

If you, through your organization or through your role as an individual leader, want to take full advantage of the opportunities presented through ambidexterity and convergence, you have to accept that you are leaving the normal/usual playing field. You are no longer playing soccer that is for sure. However, this is where clarity ends and ambiguity starts. Now what? In exploration, we want to escape the rigidities of the existing business. This means you are now venturing into the unknown. You may strike gold or you may lose. How can you do this? How can you de-risk the activities for both you and the organization?

C. K. Prahalad introduced the conceptual framework for "shaping game strategies" with the idea that you do not simply agree to play the game of soccer; you create your own game and your own rules. Now, you could change the game of soccer to include, for example, elements of American football. You can immediately see how your soccer team will look different.

Shaping game strategies are like puzzles you may recall from your childhood. You say, ok, there are 500 pieces in the box that I have to put together to recreate the picture on the box, for instance a picture of the skyline of Zürich. What do you do with the 500 pieces? You group all the blue pieces into two sections – these are pieces of blue sky and pieces of blue water. You find all the corner pieces, select the pieces related to bridges, churches, and buildings. After a few hours you will have recreated the picture on the box, and I'm sure you remember the sheer joy when the last piece fits right in its place.

Shaping game strategies also involve the painstaking process of putting many pieces together like in the puzzle example. The only – and quite important – difference is that the box comes without a picture!

Now, how can you create a puzzle without a picture? You cannot. The way out: You have to create your *own* picture for your organization, for yourself, for the people/organizations/your partners.

Shaping game strategies are not about forecasting (our market share in 1–2 years from now) or predicting the future. They are about having a "point of view." In shaping game strategies there is no picture on the box, you are only given the pieces of the puzzle and you have to identify any missing pieces. Therefore, the key challenge is to create "a picture."

In a recent meeting, bringing together key stakeholders for the next phase in health care, a French participant requested that for the next meeting: "We need to create a Vision." This is usually a very abstract request – yet, very real in shaping game strategies.

The starting point: To have a point of view. This can be a hypothesis for what is going to happen. Take Steve Jobs when Apple announced the launch of the iPad. People said, "We already have a laptop/PC and a smartphone – what do we need to have an iPad for?" Steve Jobs went ahead anyway, and the rest is history. He had a point of view and the necessary alliances with various partners to deliver. But, to do so, you need to have the confidence to move past the idea stage.

Step 1: Have a point of view, create a picture, and put a stake in the ground.

Step 2: Assess the capabilities required to deliver against the picture; that is, identify the pieces of the puzzle.

Step 3: Identify those pieces of the puzzle you own or already have access to.

Step 4: Identify the missing pieces and potential owners of these missing pieces.

Step 5: Persuade the individual players to help build your picture and to participate.

Having a point of view versus prediction

In shaping game strategies one has to let go of some traditional measures such as market share. In a market that does not yet exist, it is by definition impossible to measure market share. Therefore, shaping game strategies are based on:

- Having a point of view.
- Not having all pieces to the puzzle in one organization.
- Identifying missing capabilities.
- Networking; partnering with other organizations that can bring in the missing capabilities.

Definition of innovation: Doblin

Most people make the instinctive link "innovation = new product". Indeed in most companies "innovation" is associated with R&D. The Institute of Design in Chicago developed a model of ten types of innovation – product innovation being only one of them. The Doblin Group commercialized the approach to push for innovation in areas such as the business model (how do we get paid?), networking partners, processes, and how we go to market.

The original model as published in the *Harvard Business Review* (Carr, 1999) distinguishes the following ten types of innovation:

- **Business model** – how are you being paid? (Upfront, e.g. Dell; annually, e.g. insurance; follow-on business, e.g. Gillette).
- **Networking** – new partners from outside your company or industry. For example, universities, research centers, start-ups, and so on.

- **Enabling processes** – processes, which support your core activities through customer relationship management tools, people development initiatives, IT support, and so on.
- **Core processes** – depending on your industry, this reflects the heart of the business (manufacturing, sales, services).
- **Product performance** – making the existing product better, faster, and more appreciated by the customer.
- **Product system** – how is the product embedded (like a Lego system) in a web of other products and services.
- **Service** – the services which support the customer through the purchasing decision and provide after sales support.
- **Channel** – how do you reach your end users (directly, through retailers, via the sales force, with third parties, etc.).
- **Brand** – the name of what you are offering. How is it positioned (vis-á-vis the competition) in the mind of the customer.
- **Customer experience** – the way your customer interacts with your product or service. How to turn a transaction into a relationship with your customer (networks, communities, co-creation).

This model has been applied in numerous industries such as banking, steel, pharmaceuticals, and even law firms!

Why is it so powerful? It forces individuals from the same company or industry to share examples and to create a common language around what they mean by innovation.

For example, it is easily possible for a group of executives to agree on an innovation landscape, to describe in which types of innovation they observed with the highest levels of innovation activity in their business in recent years. Based on that analysis, it is then possible to identify opportunities for innovation going forward.

A typical innovation landscape as produced by executives in an innovation workshop is displayed in Figure 1.1. The example chosen represents a very typical pattern: In many businesses it emerges that the majority of innovation activity is focused on product innovation and process innovation.

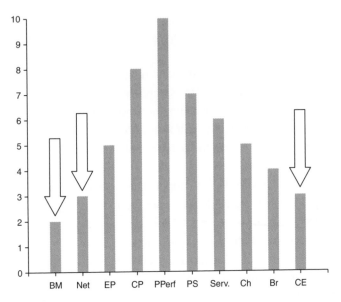

FIGURE 1.1 / **Example of Innovation Landscape**

The often-neglected areas are business model innovation, networking, and customer experience. Therefore, executives looking at the innovation landscape in their industry will immediately see the opportunity going forward: The arrows in Figure 1.1 indicate types of innovation so far neglected in the whole industry.

The insights from having generated such an innovation landscape include:

- Innovation in only one of the ten types can easily be copied.
- Combining three to five types of innovation simultaneously is key to success – it is difficult to copy. Successful innovations that we admire, such as Nespresso or say the iPad, include a number of types of innovation that were implemented simultaneously.

The link innovation – ambidexterity

The analysis of the innovation landscape in your market will show peaks and valleys. The peaks identify the highest levels of activities, for example, in product performance and core process innovation. The peaks show where everyone else is innovating. The consequence for your organization is that you have to continue to innovate there also.

However, it is very likely that these innovation activities in the peaks will be "exploitation" projects. Exploration projects would then be targeting the "valleys" in the innovation landscape – purposefully addressing types of innovation, which for some reason have so far been overlooked.

Who leads, who follows? (fast second)

As we have seen, ambidexterity works at two levels, exploitation and exploration. Exploitation, the continuous improvement, is well established in large organizations. For the large organizations the challenge is more in the exploration area. Exploration is risky – it is not clear when there is a common standard, and you have to manage partners internally and externally.

Start-up companies usually do not have that worry. For them it is a one-way street: They either make it or fail. This clear focus is then driven by the potential for personal gain (material/reputational) but also driven by their investors. This forces start-ups to display the agility to find partners, finance, and large organizations as potential integrators. Therefore, for them the choice is clear – they will have to lead from the front.

In large corporates the situation is different. Yes, they have their core markets. There they have to fight for growth and market share. A lot of energy is expended on innovation in the daily fight for supremacy in this core market. Exploration of new opportunities beyond the core market is then an extra on top. Organizations have to find the energy in both resources and talent for the exploration efforts; then they have to make clear choices. Where is worth exploring? Where should be avoided?

In the book *Fast Second*, strategy professor Costas Markides argues, with co-author Paul Geroski, that large organizations may be better suited for a strategy of observation/scouting rather than leading from the front (Markides and Geroski, 2004). The logic is that large organizations are notoriously bad at innovating beyond their current industry boundaries. So, why bother? Why waste the energy of the organization on something that it will not be good at anyway? Instead, Markides and Geroski argue, the organization should develop two sets of capabilities:

1) **Scouting:** This is to purposefully observe any emerging technologies, trends, and interesting start-up companies. This should be done from a strategic perspective, both from a customer perspective (how do customer preferences shift) and from a capability perspective, identifying specific targets (technologies/companies) that should be purposefully integrated.

2) **Scaling:** Once identified, specific scouting targets can then be bought and integrated into the organization. The muscles of a large organization can then be brought into play: Scaling across markets and geographies.

The benefits for a large organization of applying the strategy of "fast second" are quite compelling:

- Staying focused on managing the core business without being distracted by exploration projects in unchartered territories.
- Not wasting resources on exploration projects with a high rate of risk.
- Avoiding the costs of war for standards. That is, by waiting until the dust settles and standards in converging markets are being shaped.

Of course there are counter arguments to the fast second strategy:

- Is your organization ready to deal with the "not invented here" syndrome? The logic of the fast second strategy depends on the speedy integration of scouting targets developed outside the organization. For instance, in a large family-owned organization carrying the family name, the culture could be to simply reject anything that comes from outside "the family."
- With a quasi-outsourcing of exploration, what is the impact on agility in the core business? Will the rest of the organization remain awake enough for changes in the market place?

• How well are the scouting experts accepted by top management and by the rest of the organization? The risk here is the delegation to a small team in corporate strategy, for instance, may sound like ivory tower thinking – easily ignored for lack of practicality by both top management and line managers.

However, the main argument from an ambidexterity perspective lies outside the organization. It is based on *access* to the scouting targets. Once the scouting experts have identified the right targets, is the organization then actually ready to act? Here it is not about speed but much more about already established networking agreements that the scouting targets may have to honor. In fact, the organization may find itself already "locked-out."

The real danger is not in being second, but in being a "slow second." We have seen recently many examples of this, including Blackberry and Nokia, among others.

The real danger is not in being second, but in being a "slow second"

Drivers for Ambidexterity

It is global mega trends such as aging population, green energy, mobility, and accessibility that drive ambidexterity. Established industries are being eroded, business models are becoming obsolete, and new contenders are creating new markets. Global mega trends are well described in other publications. In this book, I will only focus on two examples in more detail: Aging population and DNA Analysis.

Example: Aging population

In August 2014 the rating agency Moody's predicted that by the year 2020 the number "super-aged" nations, in which more than 20 per cent of the population is older than 65, will have increased to 13 (*Financial Times*, 2014). As individuals get older and continue to lead independent lives into very old age, new market opportunities arise. Take pharmaceuticals, most of the innovation effort is directed towards R&D – creating better drugs with ever better efficacy. As people get older there may be greater demand for these drugs.

However, new areas for innovation arise. As the health care providers in most countries try to limit the cost of prescription drugs, they will actually want to ensure that a drug prescribed is actually taken. It is estimated that up to 50 per cent of drugs prescribed end up unused around the world. It is no wonder that the health care providers push the pharmaceutical industry to demonstrate not just the efficacy of a drug, but also when and if it is indeed taken.

Here the new exploration opportunities kick in: Smart packaging may create drug containers equipped with chips that send a message to the prescribing doctor or to a caring relative that indeed the drug has left the container at the prescribed time. That would certainly provide reassurance that the drug has left the package, which is already an interesting step forward. However, this is not a guarantee that the drug has actually been administered. Therefore, for critical cases additional information via diagnostic patches on the body of the patient can ensure that the drug has, as intended, reached the body at the specified time.

Let's look at the previous example. How many different capabilities were required? Sure there are pharmaceuticals, there are also packaging, sensors, ICT to transmit the data, Apps on the smartphone, and so on. Somehow, all these various capabilities have to be harnessed. Who should take the lead? It is a clear cross-industry opportunity. Every player in one industry will have its own capabilities and boundaries and restrictions, because it involves capabilities outside that industry's "core competences."

Example 2: DNA analysis: Towards the segment of one

The progress that has been made in analyzing individual DNA codes is breathtaking. Whilst in 2001 it was available for US$ 30,000, today organizations such as 23andMe in the US or bio.logis in Germany offer the service for US$ 60.00 and Euro 300.00 respectively. These price points place this valuable individual information at the fingertips of a large number of the world's population.

Now, the uptake of these services has been limited by general awareness, data security issues, and a general "I'd rather not know" attitude. The people who so far have embraced the opportunity of their own DNA analysis fall into two extreme categories: The very sick and the very healthy. The very sick see tremendous value in understanding better their drug sensitivity depending on their DNA. A drug sensor can immediately identify which elements of a drug cocktail, for say a cancer patient, can be potentially harmful. At the other end of the spectrum, for example, those people training for a triathlon or climbing a big mountain, there is also great interest. Information on a person's DNA will reveal which type of training, say weights vs cardio-vascular exercise, will give them the best preparation to achieve their goals. Equally important is nutrition: A DNA analysis may reveal great insights into what type of nutrition and in what quantities is most appropriate for the body's optimum performance.

Although the acceptance of DNA analysis has been strongest at both ends of the bell curve, the biggest opportunity lies in the middle – the normal people. In 2013 an example of this trend was observed in the use of wristbands not only by triathletes but by the health-conscious in business. If it is acceptable in a business context to show up in shirt and tie and a wristband, something is shifting. It becomes a statement: "I care for my health," "I am a responsible citizen because I monitor my activities around exercise and sleep." However, it also implies: "This is my personal data, I own it. I may share it selectively with a selected few, like family and friends, but I am in charge."

If you connect the potential fad of the wristbands with the opportunities of the DNA analysis, something significant happens. With a DNA analysis the individual has his/her baseline. As any new scientific insights around the specific DNA constitution become available the individual can be alerted to these new insights. This enables that person to then obtain additional professional information around the consequences on nutrition, exercise, or other general personal behavior. However, with the wristband technologies some smart on-going diagnostics can be achieved. As a consequence of this, the individuals are more than ever in charge of their own data. Of course, individuals will seek out advice because the data may be too overwhelming. However, people now have access to more data and insights about themselves than ever before.

How will that data be used? Individuals have always felt unique. With DNA analysis, that uniqueness can now be proven. Tracking devices can be used to control and measure the specific behavioral parameters relevant to each individual. This will change people's relationships to:

• Doctors.
• Fitness centers.
• Nutrition providers.
• Insurance providers.

This will lead to the segment of one and will have ramifications for a number of industries. Yes, in pharmaceuticals we already talk about "personalized medicine." However, in many other industries segmentation in its traditional style prevails – people like you. Nutrition and insurance are two industries in which senior executives will tell you that they know their customers. Of course a long tradition of effective market research has uncovered very powerful insights.

However, in nutrition the manufacturers do not know their customers by name. The retailers, through their loyalty cards, may do so. The manufacturers often are at the mercy of the retailers to share that information.

Let me give you an example. Whether Jens Maier bought a Pepsi or a Coca-Cola beverage today is unclear to the manufacturers. However, the retailer – Wal-Mart, Tesco, Migros, or Co-op – would know. In insurance the risk models are also based on people like you. Actuarial science still has quite a challenge to face in dealing with individual, event specific risk.

With the segment of one we can expect a whole set of different discussions with our customers. They will no longer be content with an offer for "people like you" – they will want to have the product or service packaged "for me." Nespresso shows how to do it.

The Ambidextrous Organization – Summary of Strategic Challenges

The main strategic challenges for ambidextrous organizations such as Nestlé, Philips, and the Thai organization is to make the strategic choice: Where do we want to innovate, where do we have to innovate?

The Doblin model with the definition of ten types of innovation usually provides a very good starting point to determine for the business:

- Which types of innovation have received the highest attention in our industry? The outcome is a picture of the innovation landscape.
- Now, which types of innovation should we focus on?

In most industries, the innovation landscape will demonstrate that the focus has been on product innovation and process innovation. It is clear that if all your competitors are innovating in these spaces you also have to be active there. This is using one hand, the exploitation hand. You take existing products and processes and make them better. As much as you have to do that, it is usually very difficult to obtain real competitive advantage, but you have to do so in order to stay in the game, to offer the "table stakes."

The analysis of the innovation landscape will also reveal the "valleys," the types of innovation that are being underutilized in your industry. Candidates for these types of innovation oftentimes include:

- Networking – partnering with organizations inside or outside our industry;
- Business model – here defined as "how do we get paid?" The revenue model; and
- Customer experience.

The analysis is very fast, the implementation of the insights generated very challenging. Here we are now talking about exploration. These areas are the clear targets for exploration projects.

The issue is how to address the exploration projects:

- Internally we will have to cover marketing, finance, and legal.
- The decision to appoint a project leader; what is his/her background, expertise?
- How do we run such a multi-functional team?
- Ambiguity; how can we launch a project without knowing the exact return on investment?
- Missing capabilities; where outside of our organization can we find the missing pieces to the puzzle?
- Yes, we have assembled our network partners; how can we now run the project successfully? Who does what, who gets what?
- Would it be better to be a fast second? Then at least we'll know where to go, which partner to buy, which standards to follow.

From the points above it is not difficult to deduce that ambidexterity is quite challenging. This is exactly why many organizations are playing it safe and focusing on "exploitation" projects. And yes we observe that conclusion in many organizations day in and day out. This is why so many unknown competitors can come in to disrupt existing industries and shape new markets. Tesla in the car industry and Google with its driverless car may be cases in point.

From an organizational perspective, exploration is providing a significant challenge and there are a lot of incentives to take the "do nothing" route or the presumably safe route through "exploitation." Welcome to Kodak, Nokia, and Blackberry country!

Given the organizational challenges, how can we break through the potential deadlock? It is clear from the above that individuals in organizations need to step out of their comfort zone in their roles as managers. They have to assert themselves in a leadership role.

Enter the ambidextrous leader, as we will discuss in the next chapter.

chapter 2

Leadership Challenges

Why is this Important for You and for Your Organization?

In this chapter we will highlight the leadership challenges from the perspective of the individual. As explained in the Introduction, an individual can be in the roles of:

- Architect; the strategist for change.
- Project leader.
- Implementer; the local manager in charge of applying the new process.

The focus in this chapter will be on the roles of architects and leaders, in which individuals can exercise real choices. These roles require individuals to actively exercise their leadership rather than just perform their manager role. That choice is limited for an implementer. As the recipient of the innovation, this individual will have to focus more on the managerial aspects of implementation.

The chapter will address first an important individual driver: The difference between motivation and volition. Then, for yourself it is critical to review what your personal preference is: *Intrapreneur*, shaping the future from within a solid organization or entrepreneur, setting up your own entity. For organizations it is important to understand these different roles and the challenges individuals are faced with.

Crossing the Rubicon

Heike Bruch and Sumantra Ghoshal in their 2002 article, "Beware the Busy Manager" in the *Harvard Business Review* introduced to the leadership literature a very powerful concept, which in retrospect allowed me to understand why so many innovations projects failed. They called it "crossing the Rubicon." From an academic perspective, it explains the difference between "motivation" and "volition," the willpower to focus on the implementation of a specific goal.

Since 1985 I have, in roles as varied as teacher, consultant, management developer, strategist, and capability developer, worked with thousands of executives across industries and geographies. Now, what do these executives have in common? They have all been identified as "high potentials" or "top talent."

In my academic work at Warwick Business School, University of Southern California, London Business School, and University of St. Gallen, the entry barriers for any one participant are extremely high. MBA programs at these schools are globally ranked very high, with the entry criteria to match. Executive education at these establishments is very expensive, thus forcing the corporate sponsors to really identify the most promising individuals as participants. Even in my corporate roles at both Daimler Benz and Zurich Financial Services I've had the privilege to work with the top 800 in each organization.

Therefore, for close to 30 years I had the opportunity to work with top talent. And what has been the focus of that work? Innovation and change.

Through purposeful selection, I had the chance to work with individuals who should have one thing in common: Motivation! Why? Of course, they had to fight to get onto the MBA programs; they had to endure the various organizational selection processes. As they walked into our workshops, classes, and innovation projects one thing was clear: All eyes were on them! How can you not be motivated, if you know that your colleagues, friends, and family are watching you?

Yes, indeed, it is motivation they all had in common. This was witnessed through:

- High levels of engagement in classroom sessions.
- Spending weekends away from their families to participate in innovation workshops.
- Endless idea generation sessions in the bar after work.
- Generation of very specific ideas for innovation.

In fact, endless "we should do this" and "if only top management did that" ideas were poured out.

But, what was the implementation rate of all this motivation? Very low, in fact far too low! My colleague Costas Markides also observed this low level of impact. So much so that *Fast Second* was written in response to this experience of low implementation of highly motivated ideas and individuals in large organizations.

For an illustration of the difference between motivation and volition, see the example from Zurich Financial Services.

BOX 2.1 ZURICH FINANCIAL SERVICES EXAMPLE

After four sessions of a new leadership program addressing shaping game strategies, the participating executives demanded that we not just talk about it, but do it for real. After a few days of preparation the offer was made to assemble again for three days to identify real projects. The first two days were allocated to idea generation, selection, and harnessing the ideas. Day three was dedicated to short, sharp presentations to the business development director, Mr. X. In this first workshop some seven concepts had been created.

So let us re-create the first two presentations.

Presentation 1:

"Dear Mr. X, here is the business case. The opportunity is this, the strategic impact that..."

Then the presenter paused and asked at the end of the presentation: "So, Mr. X who is taking this project forward?"

How would you have responded in Mr. X's position?

We had no reference point, since it was the first presentation in what later on would add up to more than 70 presentations over a few years.

After a few seconds of deliberation, which seemed more like minutes to everyone in the room, Mr. X responded:

> "You put all the effort in to produce in two days this compelling idea. Thank you very much. I think you should take the lead in this first phase. How can I give it to somebody else at this stage?"

Presenter: *"Ah, it is for real? I did not know..."*

Presentation 2:

> "Dear Mr. X, thank you for having provided us with a tremendous opportunity for business development. Let me tell you what my American colleague and I have decided to do: We will set up a project team in Chicago, xyz in my team has been appointed project leader. I will give 20 per cent of my time to this project. We can re-allocate resources internally so we do not need to get any extra budgets. In three months we will report back to you..."

Mr. X's reaction: stunned silence, followed by a *"great, that you have used the stage we have provided."*

What the Zurich example should illustrate is:

- Both presenters were *motivated*. They both worked hard for three days to develop their innovation concept and to present it in a very concise and appealing way.
- The difference is in the level of commitment. Clearly the second presenter displayed a much higher level of commitment.

This is where the work of Bruch and Ghoshal comes in – unfortunately after my time at Zurich Financial Services! They make a clear distinction between "motivation" and "volition." After having analyzed many innovation projects, they concluded that it was not the level of motivation that mattered, but the presence or absence of volition, the willpower.

In their book, *Beware the Busy Manager*, Bruch and Ghoshal illustrate the difference with the example of Julius Cesar and the river Rubicon. When approaching Rome with his troops Julius Caesar stopped at the River Rubicon and contemplated whether or not to cross. He knew that the very moment he crossed the river, he would be at war with Rome and that there would be no way back, he would have to win. Therefore, he contemplated, and after lengthy deliberations he decided to cross the river with the famous words *"alea iacta est"* meaning "the die is cast."

For me this is one of the most important insights around innovation: Does the leader of an innovation project display volition or only motivation?

What was the outcome of the two cases in the example illustrated above? In fact, both projects failed in the end. Not a surprise for the first presentation. Here it was very clear in retrospect that the individual displayed only motivation, but no willpower.

However, the second project also failed for various technical reasons. Volition is critical but does not eliminate the project risk.

So what does that mean?

- Motivation is not enough – if there is no volition the chance of success is very low.
- Volition is required, but by itself is not a guarantee for success. Volition is a necessary but not a sufficient prerequisite.

Here are the implications for your roles:

- As architect: You should not just rely on motivated project managers. You should purposefully identify project leaders who display volition.

- Implications for innovation processes: Create Rubicon situations! Avoid the symptom of project clutter as can be observed in many organizations. In many companies, innovation projects are being launched on a rather casual basis. Recommendation is to make it difficult, to test for the presence of volition in potential project leaders.
- As project leader: When offered a project opportunity you should put yourself at the Rubicon. Is this the right topic? Am I excited about this project? What resources do I have at my disposal? How do my stakeholders protect me?

Intrapreneur vs Entrepreneur

As organizations demand innovation from their individual leaders, this is often echoed by a call for an entrepreneurial spirit in the organization. This call from top management is understandable, but often ill conceived. Do they really want entrepreneurs, who use the organizational platform to launch their own businesses? Or, often much more likely, do they want intrapreneurs, individuals who are happy to innovate from within the organization?

Entrepreneurs and intrapreneurs constitute two different sets of individuals. In building an ambidextrous business we should be very clear about the differences. So let us have a closer look.

Entrepreneurs and intrapreneurs constitute two different sets of individuals

First, entrepreneurs and intrapreneurs have a lot in common. They want to get things done and they demonstrate drive. Both intrapreneurs and entrepreneurs would score higher than their co-workers on the points outlined in Box 2.2.

Now what is different between entrepreneurs and intrapreneurs?

Entrepreneurs have the desire to build their own businesses. They often loathe the organizational processes, calling it bureaucracy. Entrepreneurs may be the sparks to get things fired up in a large organization. However, they also may be unlikely to stay.

BOX 2.2

- I can work very long hours without getting tired to achieve my business goals.
- I feel fit and healthy.
- I set myself ambitious goals.
- I see challenges and opportunities and do not concentrate on problems.
- I feel confident in new business situations.
- I behave in very cost-conscious fashion and turn around every euro before spending it.
- I closely monitor what is going on around me.
- In most situations I have a reputation for getting things done.
- I am usually the team leader not just the team member.
- I prefer to work on different projects simultaneously.
- I quickly grasp opportunities.
- I act as an active networker.
- I am usually emotionally very strongly involved in my ideas and projects.
- I like to stretch myself beyond my comfort zone.
- I am willing to challenge the status quo and upset people in order to achieve my goals.
- I enjoy selecting and organizing new teams.
- I use my power to achieve a business goal.
- I have lots of drive and energy when I work on my business goals.
- I live a healthy life, eat healthily, and exercise regularly.
- I like to solve problems creatively and to learn from successes and failures.
- I carefully calculate the risks involved in a business venture.
- I feel restricted and retained by bureaucracy and slow decision making.
- I have a pretty good feeling for the right price of products and services.
- I pay a lot of attention to detail. I know what my priorities are when in pursuit of an idea.

- I want to influence things personally.
- I rely more on my personal analysis and intuition than on the opinion of others.
- I know whom to turn to if I need information.

Intrapreneurs get innovation implemented and embedded.

Intrapreneurs and entrepreneurs are likely to answer the points in Box 2.3 differently.

BOX 2.3

- I feel comfortable being part of a larger organization.
- I concentrate on managing the stakeholders of my projects.
- I pay a lot of attention to managing the organizational boundaries and interfaces.
- I know how my organization works and use this knowledge to achieve my goals.
- I pursue the good of the organization in my work.
- I know how to get things done in a large organization.

Innovation happens only when individuals commit themselves to a certain project. In most organizations we want to have intrapreneurs, individuals who are comfortable driving innovation from within an organization.

Track Record of Leaders: Playing the Existing Game Better

Usually, leaders in large organizations get promoted because they get things done: Managing a large re-structuring process, expanding market share, and so on. When they arrive at the top of their organization they have built up a tremendous track record in the existing business.

However, "all the achievements/learning that got me a seat at the management board may be completely irrelevant in the next phase in our industry." This statement sums up the experience of a close friend of mine who just got promoted to the top team of his organization. So, how can leaders let go of their own experience and deal with the ambiguity in the next phase in their industry?

Let us revisit the T-Model briefly mentioned in the Introduction (see Figure 2.1). Start at the bottom of the vertical axis, the moment when first leadership roles are provided by an organization. In a group of functional specialists, who gets promoted to the first leadership role? Yes, the most visible individuals: The best functional experts, the extraverts, and those with a high dose of conscientiousness. Through their technical expertise and their persuasiveness coupled with tight project planning skills they get promoted to leadership functions.

How do people move up in their careers/the vertical line? Through transactional leadership including tight goal setting, clear command, and control structures, they can get a lot done. Then re-enforcement kicks in: At the new level they will apply the same style, only on a larger stage. Why change? This is what the organization has just rewarded them for. The analogy is that individuals are moving up the functional vertical in the T-Model by way of using first a small hammer, followed by a larger hammer, and then a very large hammer as they get positive re-enforcement at every new stage. This all works as long as all the

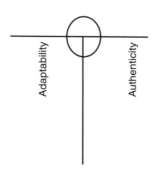

FIGURE 2.1 / The T-Model

challenges come across in the shape of a nail. Problems arise when the challenge presents itself in the shape of a screw – then even the biggest hammer will not work.

The hammer analogy is used here to refer to the dominant hand in discussing the ambidextrous personal leadership style.

What happens at the crossroad, at the intersection with the horizontal line? So, individual leaders have climbed to the top of the tree of their functional expertise. They are now the sales director, the IT director, or the finance director. The intersection of the vertical and horizontal line in Figure 2.1 represents the transition from a functional expert to a "general manager." In the role of a general manager, individuals have now to oversee other functions. For instance, based on your stellar performance as functional expert in sales you now get promoted to the role of commercial director, responsible for both sales and marketing. Now, with your strong technical expertise in sales, your track record, and a leadership style dominated by clear goal setting, telling people exactly what to do, and possibly also based on an outgoing, extraverted personality, you arrive in your new role as commercial director.

The sales people will be all right with your style, the challenge will be how to lead the marketing people. What will they say if you come along with a leadership style, "your hammer," dominated by telling and setting tight transactional goals? They will not respect you, because you may not have any track record in marketing. They are the functional experts and as commercial director/general manager you have to lead with the necessary respect for their achievements, in fact you need to be able to delegate.

Here we come back to ambidexterity: In your leadership career you will have been successful in developing your dominant hand, your "hammer." However, at the latest in general manager roles you should have developed the understanding of when it is right to use the other hand. In this example, the commercial director will only be successful if she/he can lead the marketing people on a delegation basis, rather than a command and control basis.

Now, this may seem to be all very obvious, so why talk about it here? Obvious it may be, but it constitutes a real challenge. Indeed, this is exactly the area on which the majority of in-house corporate programs at business schools focus: The transition from functional manager or leader to general management. Why are companies so concerned about this transition? We have all heard the anecdote about promoting the best sales person to sales manager, only to lose the best sales person and gain a bad manager.

Numerous studies, in particular from the Center for Creative Leadership (Leslie & Van Velsor, 1996), point out that this particular transition is mired with derailment. Depending on which study you choose, the derailment quota of those individuals making the transition from functional to general manager is between 40 and 50 per cent.

Statistics is one thing, working with real people is another. Imagine a classroom of say 40 top bankers in London, New York, Hong Kong, Singapore, and Zürich. These individuals have worked hard for many years to make their mark as functional specialists. Now they have been selected to be groomed for general management roles. Are they motivated? Of course! Are they proud to belong to this exclusive group of top talent? Of course! Are they honored by the fact that either the CEO or a top regional leader will meet them? Of course! Now, when you look at this group of 40 people and you know that the statistics will predict that about 20 of these highly skilled, motivated individuals will derail, I ask myself, what are the sources for derailment?

When I ask a group of senior executives whether they ever had a bad manager, nearly all the hands go up! Most people at some stage in their career have been exposed to a bad manager. When I ask what a bad manager consists of, brainstorming kicks in, only limited by the flip chart paper available: takes all credit, spineless, unethical, not consistent, micro manager, and on and on.

What is interesting, are the attributes identified. I always ask people: "What is the pattern you can see in this list?"

After a stunned silence, the first ideas come in: behaviors, personality.

Then, the follow-up question: "What is missing on this list?" Functional know-how.

So what does that mean for our discussion on ambidexterity:

- Individual leaders matter: Someone has to take the lead to run with an innovation project.
- Leaders develop their own dominant hand in their leadership style, early in their career.
- Within the functional area of expertise the leader can achieve a lot with his/her dominant hand.
- In general management roles leaders fail if they only rely on their dominant hand – they have to become ambidextrous leaders.
- Ambidexterity: "Exploitation" – a lot can be achieved inside a functional area alone; be it R&D, sales, marketing, and so on. "Exploration" is different: Here we need to bring cross-functional expertise to the table – very similar to general management.

Role of Personality

In the 1930s researchers (Allport & Odbert, 1936) found more than 4,000 adjectives to describe another person. The essence of their approach was the idea that if we want to understand something about another person, the language will have developed words for it. Now more than 4,000 words may be interesting, but not very helpful if you want to build a robust view on personality. So, after an initial check for synonyms (meaning the same thing) and antonyms (meaning the opposite), quite a few statistical approaches such as factor and cluster analyses had to be applied to come up with the big five.

- Neuroticism.
- Extraversion.
- Openness to change.

- Conscientiousness.
- Agreeableness.

Please note that these big five were not developed to describe leaders, managers, or executives but for "normal people," normal citizens, initially in the US. Only much later, in the 1990s, was this concept applied to the managerial world and embedded in the leadership literature (Costa & McCrae, 1992).

Meanwhile, more than 80 years of experience with the big five personality traits is available. Some conclusions include the following:

- Personality develops early, say in to your late teens.
- Personality remains remarkably stable over time; absent of any life changing events peoples' scores have remained remarkably stable over time.
- Preference for behavior; your dominant hand as a person.

As we have seen above in the example of bad managers, executives may become the victims of their own success. Mainly because they cannot add to the "hammer" the other leadership styles required such as delegation.

Your signature: In fact it is like the example in the Introduction where signing your name you intuitively put the pen in your dominant hand. But, when is it time to put the pen in the other hand?

The leadership challenges based on personality do have an impact on a person's ability to be an ambidextrous leader. For instance, in exploitation projects you will get a lot done if you display extraverted behavior coupled with a high level of conscientiousness. You will set clear goals and milestones and will monitor progress closely.

In an exploration project, where you often encounter cross-functional teams it is important to use your "influencing" style. You may not be able to rely on your organizational power to achieve the exploration project's objective. Therefore, your actual behavior should display higher levels of, say, agreeableness or openness to change than you actually have. This is where the analogy of "putting the pen in the other hand" comes back in.

Adaptability/Choice

Here is a critical point: Your personality may stay stable over your career, therefore your *preference for behavior* may stay stable.

Now, as a leader you will have a preference for behavior. For example, as an extraverted person you may want to structure a meeting. But your good intentions may equally be perceived by the team members as "domineering." So how do you get the best out of your team members? Especially those who may be far less extraverted or even introverted?

This is where adaptability comes to play. Your preference for behavior may be to structure, to dominate the meeting. But, you have a choice: you can either go with your preference for behavior or at the other extreme, deliberately decide to hold back and allow the other participants the space they require to get their important perspectives heard.

This is what adaptability is all about: To understand what your preference for behavior is and then to deliberately decide which actual behavior to display.

To stay with the analogy: You may have the preference to place the pen in your dominant hand, but you deliberately use the other hand. Very difficult to do, but it puts you in command and, at best, avoids derailment.

Authenticity

The T-Model not only promoted the idea of adaptability but also of authenticity. Now, if I am so adaptable so that I can carefully adapt my preference for behavior to any new situation, is there not a danger that other people will think I am a fake – that I move direction according to the direction of the wind? Authenticity is critical. You cannot be like a leaf in the wind.

Adaptability is a question of choice: Do I go with my preference for behavior or do I do deliberately put the pen in the other hand? Preference for behavior is not an excuse for bad behavior: In MBA classes I see it all the time, some individuals want to take all the airtime in the class. Now, that is not very productive for everyone. Likewise, to say "I am an introvert, so I cannot speak in class" is not very helpful. Both the extraverts and introverts have to purposefully adjust their behavior in order to get the best outcome. Yes, they have to adapt and yes they have to stay authentic.

Transformational Leadership

In the leadership literature it is well accepted that transactional leadership styles have to be augmented with the aspect of transformational leadership. This includes the elements of:

- **Inspirational motivation:** Motivating others with an exciting vision; enthusing people emotionally; augmenting the importance of goals and tasks.
- **Idealized influence:** Communicating enthusiasm; displaying behavior with which others can identify; showing integrity at all times.
- **Intellectual stimulation:** getting people to break out of established modes of thinking; communicating new insights.
- **Individualized consideration:** Considering each employee as an individual; re-enforcing each employee individually; promoting their self-confidence.

On the topic of individualized consideration, it is important to include the model of situational leadership (Hersey & Blanchard, 1998), which identifies four types of leadership:

- Telling.
- Selling.
- Developing.
- Participating.

Now, as we go back to the T-Model (Figure 2.1) and the hammer analogy, here is the catch: As most individuals go through the vertical line they develop a certain preference of leadership style. For instance, a very common case is a young functional expert being promoted to lead his/her first project or team.

Personal Risk

Whilst everyone wants innovation, it is risky for both the organization and the individuals associated with it. With a 4–5 per cent rate of success for innovation projects in general, this is not encouraging at either the individual or the organizational level.

It is clear that the risk around exploitation projects is manageable. We are talking about continuous improvement and R&D, all within a well-known competitive space.

It is different for exploration projects; both the organization and the project leaders are entering unchartered territory. This entails additional levels of risk for both the organization and the individual.

Why would a person take on an exploration project? "Because it is cool!" Now, this is the reply of a person from generation y. "No way" would be the reply from generation x.

To illustrate the risk levels, see the example of one of my clients in a traditional industry in Box 2.4.

BOX 2.4

Powerful CEO; agreed agenda for innovation

Age groups:

- 30, yes they are hungry, joined the boring industry to make a difference.
- 40, big budgets, well educated, track record.
- 50+, been there for 20+ years.

How would you revolutionize the industry? Surely, not with the 50+ group, they missed their chance long ago. Would you pick the 30s? Yes, but… Yes they are eager, bring a fresh perspective, many new ideas… But, do they have the standing to convince the rest of the organization? Of course not.

That leaves us with the late 30s, early 40s; sure they must be our people? Indeed, here we find the individuals who have made it very successfully through the junior ranks of large organizations, people from consultancy. At this level individuals are one or two steps away from the management board – highly educated, great track record – big budgets.

What do you think? Is this the group of people to embrace ambidexterity, the joining of exploitation *and* exploration? Exploitation is much safer; we have to make the numbers next quarter.

It is quite clear what happens in an organization if the next layer after the management board of an organization does not push. Not much, or to be precise, more of the same. That is, continues improvement, cost cutting, and so on.

Why are those in the 30/40+ group not taking up the challenge? Why would they? At this stage they are one step away from the management board. They worked very hard to get into this position. The next moves have to carefully planned and executed.

Take also the personal situation. Executives are not robots; they have to look after their personal relationships, families, and so on. By the way, with individuals in their late 30s and early 40s we see a lot of young families around the world.

You can immediately see in Box 2.5 why the pressure is on for the person who has got two kids at home, and a mortgage to pay. So, as a rational individual, why would you take on an exploration project instead of picking a safe exploitation project? At a personal level, the risk to engage in innovation projects around "playing the existing game better" is significantly lower than the risk in "shaping game" projects. Therefore, surprisingly the up and coming stars in a large organization may be forgiven for playing it safe – betting on exploitation projects.

BOX 2.5 AN IMAGINATIVE
SITUATION

Person x, one step away from the management board, comes home to his/her partner.

"I have got two options in my organization:

1) I can restructure the country business with *xvz* consultancy.

2) I can do an innovation beyond project."

What will the partner say? What will the partner say if there are two small kids at home?

Change Management: Kotter, Urgency, Coalition

Innovation and change in large organizations will not happen without a solid leadership coalition and strong support from the top. This means that individuals very close to the top have to champion/sponsor the innovation or change. For me the most surprising failures in innovation projects over the years came from ignoring the Kotter (1996) framework for change:

1) Create a sense of urgency.
2) Establish strong leadership coalitions.
3) Create a compelling vision.
4) Communicate the vision for the change.
5) Empowering others with comprehensive options to act.
6) Generate short-term and visible successes.
7) Consolidate gains and successes.
8) Institutionalize new measures in the everyday routine.

Whether an individual with a passion for a topic or an engineer having discovered a "strong solution," everyone may stumble at the first hurdle of the Kotter change model – urgency for change. "If it is not broken don't fix it" is the usual reply from the organizational ranks as these missionaries fail to create a sense of urgency for change. Forming a guiding coalition, as a next step in Kotter's model, could be viewed as unnecessary politicking by an engineer who has developed a "strong solution." It is no surprise that these missionaries fail – although they may have had the right insight at the right time.

Summary

In order to build ambidextrous businesses, we need to have leaders inside organizations who are comfortable operating in an ambidextrous environment.

This chapter identified challenges from the leadership perspective. Here core leadership concepts were addressed in the context of ambidexterity.

The importance of volition, rather than just motivation, has been stressed here: Successful innovation projects have project leaders who display willpower once they have chosen to cross the Rubicon.

As much as many organizations like to have entrepreneurs, the reality is often that these organizations are better served by intrapreneurs. Entrepreneurs may use the organization to launch their own businesses. This by itself may not be a bad thing, as long as the organization can still benefit from a partnership in the new setting. Intrapreneurs are those individuals who have the drive to innovate, but to do that within the comfort and support of an existing, potentially large organization.

The impact of the track record of an individual was also investigated. The analogy of the T-Model was used to illustrate that leaders develop their dominant, personal leadership style as they progress in their career. When it comes to ambidexterity – the ability to run both exploitation and exploration projects – personal leadership style matters. In exploitation projects a "telling" leadership style is useful, whereas exploration projects require much more of an influencing style, as different stakeholders inside and outside the organization have to partner and to cooperate.

Personality – the preference for behavior – obviously plays a part in how an individual develops her/his leadership style. And, again, it has implications for how an individual deals with ambidexterity. For example, individuals with a high score on "openness to change" will be much more attracted to an exploration project than those with low scores. Understanding personality is an important initial insight for an individual leader. This is the basis for understanding when it is time to use the other hand in order to be successful in both exploitation and exploration situations.

Transactional leadership, the rational part, the clear goal setting, and clear follow-up, will be very important for exploitation projects. However, in exploration projects the application of transformational leadership is critical. Here the partners in the exploration project want to see the emotional side of the leader; here the importance of creating an exciting picture, a vision, is critical.

Innovation does not come without risk. So the individual propensity to accept personal risk matters. Exploration projects carry a higher risk than continuous improvement projects. There is a need to derisk the nature of exploration projects in order to win the support of individuals, who for very good personal reasons may be more risk averse than others.

One way to derisk, especially exploration projects, is the application of the Kotter change model. Here in eight clear successive steps, starting with creating a sense of urgency, then followed by creating a strong leadership coalition, the foundation is laid for harnessing and managing innovation.

3

Process challenges

Why is this Important for You and for Your Organization?

For you personally it is important to understand your role in the processes around ambidexterity: 1) architect or 2) project manager. At the organizational level the process challenge is the most important one: Does your organization differentiate in innovation processes between exploitation projects and exploration projects? If not, the architect for ambidexterity has to initiate changes at the organizational level to avoid failure for both individual project leaders and the organization as a whole.

Innovation Processes: The Innovation Funnel

For generations students and practitioners alike have used the concept of the innovation funnel. This funnel is illustrating the move through the stages of ideation, screening, and implementation. Robert Cooper (1990) has established the process in a very sophisticated way. Each stage in the process is well supported through a set of appropriate tools.

Ideation

The first phase, ideation, can be supported through a variety of creativity techniques such as brainstorming, which is well documented by Edward de Bono (1970).

Many organizations also use their own employee idea generation systems, whereby employees are encouraged to contribute ideas for innovation. The challenge for these innovation suggestions is to maintain the momentum and to demonstrate to the participating employees that the organization is indeed acting upon the suggestions made.

More recently it has become fashionable for organizations to proactively engage their customers to offer concrete ideas, often known as crowd sourcing. Good examples of this come from Starbucks and Dell. At www.mystarbucksidea.force.com and at www.ideastorm.com customers are encouraged to submit ideas and it is also demonstrated to these customers to what extend these ideas are being taken up by the organization.

In the case of Starbucks, by November 2014 some 43,000 suggestions for coffee or espresso had been submitted, around 19,000 ideas regarding the experience at Starbucks with focus on atmosphere, and some 10,000 ideas about involvement with focus on social responsibility. For Dell the number of ideas submitted stood at more than 21,000, of which more than 500 were implemented. The benefits to the organizations are obvious: The number of eligible ideas is increased dramatically, and a direct relationship with their lead customers is established.

Open innovation is another approach. One of the first platforms was InnoCentive, which allows organizations to put innovation challenges to the global Internet space and, with the help of some 200,000 solvers, try to find a solution. The solvers are incentivized by receiving the promised cash award attached to the challenge posted by an organization.

These more recent developments have increased the scope for identifying suitable ideas way beyond the traditional idea generation processes within an organization.

Screening

The second stage in the innovation funnel is screening. It usually involves two important criteria: Strategic fit and the return-on-investment (ROI) hurdle rate, the financial criterion. The strategic fit criterion checks the extent to which an idea is related to the strategic agenda of the organization. Is there a fit with the core competencies of the organization? How is this idea related to the current portfolio of innovation projects? How does it fit with the strategic intent of an organization?

As financial criterion, most organizations use the notion of a "hurdle rate." As organizations have increased their sophistication in financial management to explicitly focus on value creation, the hurdle rate ensures that only projects above a certain pre-agreed ROI threshold get started. For example, if an organization has agreed a hurdle rate of 12 per cent ROI as a threshold for starting new projects, any project proposals have to then demonstrate that this hurdle has been met.

Let us examine how as a project leader you should prepare your case to demonstrate that the hurdle rate is met. For the duration of the project you identify the cash flow based on estimates of cash outflow and inflows at certain points in time during the project. Using the discounted cash flow method you then calculate the net present value (NPV) of an investment in project x. If the NPV is positive it has been demonstrated that this project has met the hurdle rate. Therefore, the key drivers for these calculations are:

- Amounts of cash outflow.
- Expected time of outflow.
- Amounts of cash inflow.
- Expected time of inflow.
- Cost of capital.
- Hurdle rate.

So how sure can you be about the calculation? It is intuitively clear that the closer a project is to an existing product and to an existing customer base the more reliable your estimates are going to be, as you are operating in familiar territory. It is also intuitively clear that the further away a project is from existing products and existing customer bases; the more the robustness of the prediction will decrease. Therefore, as exploitation projects are so much closer to existing products and markets compared to exploration projects, the calculations for exploitation projects are much more robust.

Screening Risky Project Ideas: Monte Carlo Simulation

Monte Carlo Simulation is a very powerful technique to get a feel for the risk inherent in an innovation concept/project. Although well embedded in the literature and teaching on operations research, my personal exposure to it in the real business world in the last 30 years has been very limited. This lack of practical application is really not justified.

Especially when deciding on a complex and large investment project the Monte Carlo Simulation should be considered. Its relevance is twofold. First the technique allows you to run literally thousands of simulations of possible outcomes. In a normal scenario analysis you would consider maybe three options, such as best case, worst case, and a likely case. Therefore, the sophisticated Monte Carlo Simulation will give you a much wider option space than the three scenarios.

Monte Carlo Simulation will give you a much wider option space

Secondly, the Monte Carlo Simulation can serve as a very influential "process" tool for decision making. It forces the decision makers to spell out their assumptions about the value drivers in innovation opportunities. Also, once you have the value drivers identified it forces the decisions makers to explicitly determine the boundaries for each value driver and the associated distribution of likely occurrences. For example, the sales volume could be as low as zero or as high as a million. Secondly, the distribution matters: Is it following a bell curve with 500,000 as midpoint or is it more skewed to the left or right? Now, the process of the decision makers that leads to agreeing on the key parameters of the model is critical. In this process the differences of opinion, assumptions, and beliefs are becoming apparent.

The outcome of a Monte Carlo Simulation is therefore twofold:

- A clear result on the risk profile of the innovation decision. This is helpful when the results indicate a clear recommendation for a go/no-go decision. Alternatively, when the results shows a tight call between go and no-go, it is also very insightful to the decision makers, as it makes the case for a very rigorous decision process and in case of a go decision, indicates extra careful project monitoring.
- Clarity on the underlying assumptions about the decision. The project team can clearly spell what the key drivers are and what the range of each driver and the probability structure are. It is therefore a very powerful tool to foster group decision making. Crama et al (2007) showcase a detailed example in the pharmaceutical industry.

The example in Box 3.1 illustrates the potential of the Monte Carlo Simulation when it was used to great effect working with a group of executives in the energy business. The company had for many months debated the investment into two potential projects both with a substantial level of investment and associated high risks.

BOX 3.1 CASE EXAMPLE: THE ENERGY BUSINESS

The company decided to use the format of a one-week executive program for the top 20 senior executives as a way to create a second opinion on the viability of these projects. Sponsors were the CEO and the Head of Corporate Development, who in preparation had collected a lot of the relevant data and potential background sources.

The five days were used as follows:

Day one: Introduction by the CEO to set the scene in terms of expectations including the final presentations and discussions expected on day five. This was followed by the introduction of the two projects by the director corporate development. The 20 executives in attendance were allocated to one of four teams, allowing for a red team and a blue team for each project.

Next came strategy input by an expert faculty member, who was covering key concepts in value creation and the role of competitive advantage. This was followed by the application of the strategy concepts to the projects. The expert faculty acted in a role as advisor to the teams, challenging assumptions.

Day two: Finance input around key concepts like net present value, value creation, and techniques to assess the viability of projects. First approaches to apply financial concepts to projects. The expert faculty member acted as advisor, challenging assumptions.

Day three: Decision making; key concepts such as intuition and the process of decision making. First was the application to projects, building on the financial analysis; second was the framing of the decision with the support of the expert faculty member.

Day four: Preparing the case. Introduction to the Monte Carlo Simulation and case work. Identification of the key drivers for value creation and attachment of a possible value range for each driver and a probability curve. This was followed by running Monte Carlo Simulations for each team a number of times, to test for robustness of assumptions and the interaction of the drivers for value creation. Finally, preparing the case presentation.

Day five: Case presentation and discussion with the CEO and director of corporate development. Case presentations addressed both the strategic validity and financial validity of the projects. All presentations also clearly spelled out the assumptions across key value drivers.

Project one

Red team 30 minutes: Blue team 30 minutes.

Recommendation: Both groups recommended to go ahead, as the Monte Carlo Simulations indicated a very safe bet.

The discussion: All the senior executives in the room felt that their gut instinct had been confirmed and that the recommendations were in line with the current direction for the ultimate decision for go/no-go. However, everyone appreciated the process of systematically identifying the value drivers and attaching a range of possible outcomes and assigning appropriate probability curves.

Project two

Red team 30 minutes: Blue team 30 minutes.

Recommendation: The red team rejected the recommendation of the blue team to go ahead. These two teams had the most difficult task. After a long investigation and re-investigation the Monte Carlo analyses in one case, the blue team, showed a value of 53, indicating go ahead; in the case of the red team a value of 47 was shown, to reject. The CEO summarized the discussion:

> "Now I fully understand why we have been finding it so difficult to make a decision in the last few months."

Process observation: The participants experienced for one week the exposure to key concepts, created a common language, and in a structured fashion explained and debated their assumptions. This was a process applied to projects with very high investment exposure and significant levels of risk attached. However, everyone admitted that usually these big-ticket decisions are made anyway – at a much lower level of sophistication.

A few weeks later the organization formally decided to invest in project one and formally rejected to invest in project two.

Implications

Even in exploitation situations, which should be less risky because we are operating in a known territory, we may have to deal with very close calls. In particular when it comes to big investments and a fairly volatile risk profile, the benefits of a rigorous process through a Monte Carlo

Simulation are high. This is less so from a number crunching perspective, but more importantly seen from a decision process perspective. We have all seen decisions being taken in the context of groupthink, without explicitly spelling out the underlying assumptions and without debating the validity of these assumptions.

The Limits of the Innovation Funnel in Exploration Projects

The application of the innovation funnel is part of most organizations' approaches to innovation. It is usually a one size fits all approach: Innovation projects are checked for strategic fit and ROI, then various project management tools are used to allow stage-gating certain milestones and so on. Now, these well-established tools are common sense and are part of many R&D processes the world over. What can be wrong with that? … It only works for "exploitation" projects!

"Exploration" projects come in with a different logic: Maybe we look for the strategic "misfit?" By definition, exploration projects are set up to innovate "beyond" what is already being done, so it is quite likely that they will be outside the realms of the current strategic focus.

ROI

How can you know the exact ROI figure at the start of an exploration project? We know our hurdle rate of say 12 per cent, therefore any smart project leader of an exploration project will pull out numbers from thin air to produce the hurdle rate. Shaping game processes work differently to exploitation processes (see Figure 3.1).

So let us examine the innovation funnel approach in the context of an exploration project.

Strategic fit

Ambidexterity by definition calls for both exploitation and exploration simultaneously. The very purpose of exploration projects is to challenge the current thinking. Therefore, any exploration project that passes the "strategic fit" requirement should be observed with suspicion. Have we really addressed the "beyond" challenge or have we just used the "exploration" project as an "exploitation" project in disguise? To put it succinctly, the first hurdle for an exploration project should be that it passes the "strategic misfit" hurdle. Only then can we be sure that we are in shaping game territory.

Now, any firm believer in the innovation funnel approach would immediately disagree with the point just made and would argue that we cannot run after any wild idea outside the strategic fit! There should of course be a solid structure behind any decision to start a project and how this new project fits into the existing portfolio of innovation projects.

Therefore, we have to clarify the meaning of the concept of "strategic misfit." It is not at all about "anything goes." Quite to the contrary! This is where the concept of the ten types of innovation and the resulting innovation landscape introduced in Chapter 1 comes in. The innovation landscapes offer us a systematic and rigorous analysis of which types of innovation our business has been investing in. Here we know already about the role of the peaks, the areas in which everyone in our industry invests. We concluded that, indeed, we have to continue to innovate here just to stay in the game. However, innovating in the peaks is not very likely to provide us with a sustainable competitive advantage. Therefore, we also – through exploration – should look at the valleys in the innovation landscape. These valleys should provide us with the distinct areas of innovation where the business/industry is either dormant or possibly negligent.

look at the valleys in the innovation landscape

Indeed, for any exploration project it should be possible to explicitly point out which types of innovation are being addressed. We also discussed the criteria for selecting exploration projects, namely the number of innovation types addressed and the importance of weaving strong connections between these distinct types.

So, in a nutshell: What has this got to do with the strategic misfit and the potential challenge of "anything goes?" The innovation landscape analysis provides you with the structure, the scaffolding for exploration. This is a very rigorous and structured approach, going well beyond any wild and potentially unstructured brainstorming ideas.

Therefore, any strategic misfit argument for a proposed project should be explicitly supported by evidence of which types of innovation are being purposefully connected, to address the valley in the current innovation landscape.

What about ROI?

So let us re-examine the drivers for the ROI calculations:

- Amounts of cash outflow.
- Expected time of outflow.
- Amounts of cash inflow.
- Expected time of inflow.
- Cost of capital.
- Hurdle rate.

At the start of an exploration project we are only certain about the cost of capital and the associated internal hurdle rate. At the beginning it is very unlikely that we fully understand the cash outflows or the cash inflows and at which exact moment in time these become prevalent. If at the start of an exploration project you force project leaders to produce these numbers, they will do it. However, how much trust do you have in these numbers? How much faith do the project leaders have in these numbers? Exactly, very little!

So how can we deal with this challenge? Very simply – just do not do it! Do not ask at the start of an exploration project for the ROI. Now, here is the critical difference between exploitation and exploration processes: For exploitation processes you have to have a clear answer to the ROI question. Do not start an exploitation project without having ensured that the ROI expectations can be met.

For exploration projects it is the opposite. Do not ask the ROI question at the start of a project; ask it at the end. This is the time when you can investigate a prototype. The decision to accelerate or to kill the prototype is very much dependent on the business case presented. That business case, based on the prototype, should have two components:

- Address the strategic fit – the fit within the current strategic agenda – or have a good story as to why the strategic misfit is important.
- ROI: Given the prototype, our story, and the financial calculations, the business case: Shall we accelerate this project or shall we kill this project?

Exploitation vs Exploration Kill/Accelerate

For exploration projects a different process is required: A short – say three-month long – phase allows the development of a prototype, the look and feel of the anticipated solution. Part of that phase is the feasibility: Can we find networking partners? What exactly is the business model? What is the ROI? At the end of this three-month period what should be the

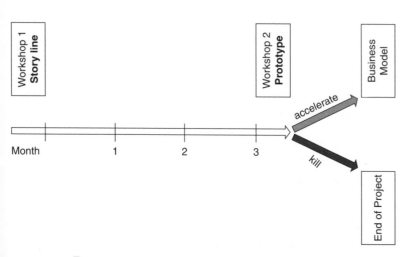

FIGURE 3.1 / Shaping Game Projects/Exploration Prototyping

business case: Accelerate – or kill? If the answer is accelerate, then the normal funnel process can kick in.

Project Teams

Most innovation projects, be they exploitation or exploration, will require the expertise from different perspectives, and possibly different functional areas. Therefore, innovation projects involve teams of people, in which each individual is expected to contribute from his/her perspective and functional expertise.

Over the years, for exploitation projects the necessity and benefits of cross-functional teams have been highlighted. This has successfully been done in the car industry, as witnessed by the fact that some eight car companies show up in the top 20 most innovative organizations. In the past it was the stage-gating: From R&D to manufacturing, to sales. Now, simultaneous engineering has allowed for much faster cycles and avoids risky handovers between departments.

What is really impressive in the car industry is the number of new permutations of models and the simultaneous reduction in R&D cycle times. In these project teams the roles and responsibilities are clear and the individuals know that for a significant length of time they will be part of this project – for example, 15 months. Similarly, an exploitation project such as introducing a new IT system – SAP, for example – will take some 12 months and requires a solid project structure around a cross-functional team supporting the project leader, who comes from IT in most cases.

In these exploitation projects, with the significant investments and a significant timeframe attached, it is worth investing in turning these teams into high performance teams.

Examples of high performance teams usually include firefighters, hospital emergency rooms, Formula 1 pit-stop crews, and sports teams. To reach the level of mutual understanding and process optimization required within these teams, a lot of time and effort is needed to ramp up the team performance into the "high performance" territory. For these teams it is still a good guideline to follow the Tuckman (1965) model of team phases.

Forming: The identification of the talent and individuals required.

Storming: The process of articulating mutual expectations and expertise; jockeying for roles and responsibilities.

Norming: The rules of engagement, how do we work together, what are the team's values, and how do we deal with value violations?

Performing: How you deliver on the project expectations, the actual collaboration required. How do you deal with setbacks?

For the duration of the project it is very likely that you will have to revisit the previous stages. This may be due to some members leaving the team, creating the necessity to integrate new team members. Also, you may have to revisit the norming stage when you discover that during the performing phase too many frictions occur, which may have to be addressed in a new norming session to introduce possibly additional values or norms for value enforcement.

Finally, in exploitation projects the team members are allocated mainly on a full-time basis, or at least on the basis that they commit a significant proportion of their time to the project.

All of the previously mentioned aspects about exploitation projects are deeply embedded in the organization's culture and more importantly in the minds of all the stakeholders. Therefore, when the organization is embarking on the idea of an exploration project, the key assumptions in stakeholders' minds are:

- 12–15 month timeframe.
- Full-time project leader; team members committed to 60–100 per cent of their time.
- Significant resources spent.

These assumptions serve indeed as the orthodoxies, the strong beliefs that will govern the way ambidexterity can be implemented in the organization.

TABLE 3.1 Comparison: Exploitation – Exploration

Exploitation	Exploration
12–15 month timeframe	3 month timeframe
Full-time project leader and team	Part-time project leader and working group
Significant resources spent	Tight exploration budget
Prototype: Physical product	Prototype: "Beyond" products

With these assumptions, orthodoxies related to innovation projects, it is normal for potential sponsors of an exploration project to raise their hands in despair "No, please do not do this on top of our already very busy agenda – we need to stay focused to deliver against our objectives according to the budget and strategic plan."

However, as Table 3.1 shows, many successful exploration projects have challenged all these orthodoxies:

Timeframe: It is possible within three months to create a prototype and to address the potential business case for this prototype. Please remember that the notion of the prototype has changed, we are looking for "beyond" concepts. Based on the business case for the prototype a decision to accelerate or to kill the project can be taken.

Project leaders/team: An exploration project can and should be done on top of the normal business commitments. The exposure for the individual leader should provide enough incentive for a top talent, with high potential to go the extra mile. For a member of the top talent group the exploration project can serve as a significant development activity to get additional exposure across the functional departments and to hone the competence of "influencing without power." As for the project team members, they are there to provide functional expertise and political commitment. This has to be done on a limited time commitment as part of their normal cross-functional "good citizen" responsibilities.

Resources: An exploration project focuses on the "beyond" aspects, that includes "beyond" R&D. Therefore, any references to the normal R&D budget expectations are not helpful. A prototype developed in the exploration phase should involve developing the story about the business concept. What is the business model? Who are the potential networking partners? Addressing these fundamental questions does not require a significant budget. For all of these activities the financial budgets can be reduced to things such as travel budgets, lawyers' fees to check IP and partnership issues, and possibly expert consultants. Many successful exploration projects have used surprisingly few resources. The power is much more driven from the project leader's desire to shape something new and to create the necessary leadership coalition inside and outside the organization.

The Link to Leadership Development Processes

Successful exploration projects will have covered at least three to five types of the ten types of innovation. This means that a successful project should have input from three to five different disciplines or organizational departments. Where should the project leader come from? How can she/ he identify and commit the other (part-time) team members? How can the project leader manage the multi-disciplinary team?

Exploration projects often provide a platform for emerging leadership talent. Hence, it is not surprising that organizations often use the leadership development process purposefully to provide project exposure. The leadership and development experts even have a term for it: action learning.

Over the years I have been regularly surprised at how individuals have used exploration platforms for their own career progression. Sure, it is normal that top talent is identified and subsequently promoted. There is one example that I have followed over the years, albeit from a distance.

There was a very young person from a remote business unit who had not finished all the normally required degrees but through sheer determination managed to get himself into the innovation program of the organization.

During an exploration project he used the three months to truly impress his senior executive sponsor, gaining corporate wide contacts and delivering impressively. Coming in from almost obscurity, he subsequently was given greater responsibility. I noticed him afterwards on two occasions in the business press. First, he featured as the project leader when the organization moved into a much-publicized operational problem. As a project leader he successfully solved complex problems in which he had to engage numerous functions and departments – whilst the organization and their customers were watching. His second press appearance came when, thereafter, he left the organization to take on the CEO role in an organization deeply involved in a turn-around case.

From a personal career progression perspective, exploration projects are a great opportunity to gain visibility inside the organization, and with potential organizational networking partners. The additional benefit is that the individual can use the exploration project as a low-risk environment to practice influencing skills, in fact to learn how to "influence without power."

Strategic Planning/Budgeting vs Spontaneous Exploration Processes

The fall of every calendar year is, for many organizations, budget time. During that period, budget holders fight for the resources available in the following calendar year.

In parallel, and usually well aligned with the budgeting process, the strategic planning process takes place. It ensures that the direction of the organization is shaped through a three to five year perspective. As part of both the budgeting and the strategic planning processes, the activities for the next calendar year are clearly fixed; all the exploitation efforts are covered when, in December, the strategic plans and the budgets are finally approved.

How do exploration projects feature inside this? Not at all, or at least very little! Think about the logic. As a budget holder you have to anticipate in September of the current year that in, say, August next year someone in your department will want to run an exploration project. There is no indication for it today; the logic for the exploration project may only build up during the first few months of the following year.

The implications for exploration projects are clear: They rarely get budgeted for in the normal budgeting process. The need for exploration projects does not follow the logic of the budgeting process. The normal pattern for most exploration projects is as follows:

- At some point during the calendar year the need for a specific exploration project appears.
- Given that it is usually a spanning opportunity, it is unclear who should fund the project. One thing is sure, no department will have budgeted for it.
- Enter the sponsor: Only a senior executive acting as a sponsor will have the political clout to fund the exploration directly or will have the power to "request" contributions from budget holders and to re-allocate some budget funds.

Summary

In this chapter we addressed the processes around innovation and for ambidexterity in particular. The challenge for both organizations and their leaders is to distinguish between exploitation and exploration processes. In many organizations this distinction is not being made and instead a "one size fits all" method is practiced. This means the process, already well practiced in exploitation, is then also applied to exploration opportunities. This means the innovation funnel concept is applied, asking for strategic fit and ROI at the very beginning.

In this chapter, we made a case for treating exploration projects differently and not applying the innovation funnel at the start of an exploration project. By their very nature, exploration projects are set up to innovate "beyond" – also beyond the "strategic fit" as manifested in the organization's previous year's strategic plan. As exploration projects come up as a response to changes in the environment, it is quite plausible that these changes were not anticipated in last year's strategic plan. Therefore, for exploration projects you can also provocatively request the test of "strategic misfit" as a prerequisite for starting an exploration project. Literally, only if the project passed the strategic misfit test would it be in the "beyond" territory.

Secondly, to start an exploration project with the request for an ROI statement is not logical and can even be wrong. This is obviously in stark contrast to the usual practice in exploitation projects. It is rightly usual practice to start exploitation projects only when the business case has been made and that the internal hurdle rate of, for example 12 per cent, has been met. However, at the start of an exploration project only the investment part is known, the return is unsure. This investment covers the resources required to build a prototype around which a business case can be formulated. The result of the business case will reveal the level of return expected and therefore will guide the recommendation towards a go or no-go.

In this chapter the case is made for the fact that exploration projects should be run through a different process:

- Initial short duration (approximately three months).
- Project leader and supporters engaged on a part-time basis, on-top of their normal commitments.
- Clear expectation at the beginning to develop a "kill" or "accelerate" recommendation based on business case for a prototype.

This approach is not suggesting to replace the normally well functioning funnel approach for exploitation projects. Indeed, the exploration project can be viewed as a pre-phase to the funnel concept. In case of a recommendation to accelerate the project, it can then enter the funnel process with its normal stage-gating milestone steps.

Project leaders of exploration projects are quite challenged in that they are exposed to a new territory, the requirement to harness expertise from across the organization – and to do that usually on top of their normal commitments. Therefore, oftentimes project leaders will use the exploration project as a way to gain organization-wide visibility and to hone their own leadership competencies.

Budgets for exploration projects are tricky in that they are usually not part of the organization's budgeting process. However, to obtain the budget for an exploration project in the middle of the financial year is sometimes easier than through the normal budgeting process. Now, this sounds very counter-intuitive, as most organizations are very strict with their budgeting and the associated financial processes. So why can it be "easy" to get the budget for an exploration project?

Here the nature of an exploration project comes in. Any exploration project needs a senior sponsor in the organization. As the content of an exploration project is already focusing on "beyond" opportunities and often spanning a number of functional areas in an organization anyway, a senior sponsor in the organization has to give the go-ahead and protection. If the sponsor is convinced of the importance of the exploration project, the appropriate budget will be found.

What is the impact for you in your role as architect?

- Make sure that an explicit process for exploration projects is in place.
- Identify senior sponsors inside the organization, who can act in an ambidextrous way.
- Identify talented individuals who are able and willing to lead exploration projects.

What is the impact for you in your role as project leader?

- Create an impactful story to get permission to start the exploration project.
- Find a senior sponsor for support in terms of permission, access to internal experts, and initial budget.
- Agree process with the sponsor regarding deliverables and the open case for either outcome: To kill or to accelerate after three months.

This now concludes the chapter on the challenges around processes for ambidexterity. If we have navigated these challenges successfully we then await the mindset challenges in the organization. This is the topic of the next chapter.

Mindset Challenges

Why is this Important for You and for Your Organization?

For yourself, this chapter may cause a bit of an embarrassment: "Just got caught!" However, that is the purpose, the realization that we are very easily becoming victims of our own beliefs and possible prejudices. At the organizational level the insight should be: "Yes, that is us as an organization... But then again, everyone else in our industry is doing the same..."

C.K. Prahalad, throughout his writings, has focused on the "dominant logic" (Prahalad and Bettis, 1986). Positively, the dominant logic in an organization provides the glue for the organization's culture. Negatively, the dominant logic can turn out to be blinkers, ideology, and orthodoxy as a major challenge for change in organizations. In this chapter a number of references will be made to his Prahalad's 2010 article for the *Harvard Business Review* titled "Why is it so hard to do the obvious?"

In this book so far we have already discussed the strategic, leadership, and process challenges. However, the mindset challenges are the biggest hurdle. With strategic challenges we can point to some trend studies, some

the mindset challenges are the biggest hurdle

new evidence that has just been published. With leadership challenges we can always blame it on the individual, that he/she did not get it. In process challenges it is fairly easy to fix once you realize what the issue is. However, with mindset challenges it is different: Here we are touching the essence of an organization, the history, and the pride – everything that made the organization successful. Ambidexterity explicitly challenges that mindset.

The German language offers the opportunity for addressing this topic as *Zukunft hat Herkunft*, meaning that the future depends on the past... Therefore, it matters a lot how you and the organization deal with past experiences as you are shaping the future.

Examples of Mindset Challenges

BOX 4.1 CASE EXAMPLE: INSURANCE COMPANY

With colleagues, I worked with more than 800 global executives from an insurance company on the topic of innovation in more than 30 workshops. In each workshop we used the 10 types of innovation as a starting point. In less than one hour the executives analyzed the innovation landscapes and described challenges in specific businesses, for example, car insurance in the US, household insurance in the UK, or life insurance in Singapore. They also quickly identified opportunities for innovation, the valleys in the innovation landscape.

Then we collectively asked the question: "Why has there been no innovation in these areas already?" We quickly realized that it was not just us who had not innovated in specific areas, such as the revenue model. Indeed it was the whole industry that had not innovated in the valleys of the innovation landscape.

After four workshops, we had a list of 15 beliefs around insurance. In the next 30 workshops only one or two new beliefs were added to the list. The beliefs identified proved to be robust across regions and businesses. For instance, insurance businesses for centuries have been based on actuarial tables. These tables are based on the probability that a certain event happens in a given time period, one year. Annuity matters. But what does annuity mean? It means calculating the risk on the basis of the calendar year. However, GPS technology in car insurance has made it possible to challenge that annuity thinking. All of a sudden a "pay as you drive" model is possible. This allows for a new revenue model based on the car trips you actually take, the road you are on, and the time you drive.

BOX 4.2 CASE EXAMPLE: BANKING

For many years my colleagues and I have worked with groups of participants from different national and international banks. They put together the innovation landscapes for different businesses such as retail banking in Spain, private banking in Switzerland, and specific investment banking businesses in the US and Singapore.

Individuals' beliefs turned out to be very similar in, for example, private banking. Across the globe private bankers were absolutely sure that no customers would pay for private banking advice. The revenue for the bank would have to be priced into the total package for the client. After the global banking crises these beliefs were suddenly challenged.

BOX 4.3 CASE EXAMPLE: ENERGY COMPANY

In a global organization with a much smaller workforce of something like 4,000 people my colleagues and I worked with the top 100 on strategy, finance, leadership, and innovation. We purposefully looked at the beliefs in the business. Again, it turned out to be very similar across geographies and across levels of management. The top management team of the organization took a summary of the beliefs and discussed these in the management team. They realized how much these deeply embedded beliefs could jeopardize the implementation of their already ambitious strategic agenda. However, the management team also realized that by purposefully challenging these beliefs a whole host of new opportunities could be imagined. These opportunities were then subsequently pursued in dedicated innovation workshops.

Out Of the Box vs Orthodoxies

Many books on innovation have focused on the importance of creativity. A good example is the work of Edward de Bono (1970). Many generations of executives have been trained in his methods to "think outside the box."

Ok, thinking "out of the box" sounds exciting, but let us first understand what is in the box. Here we are looking at the DNA code of an organization, the past successes, the joint experiences of failure, our understanding of what makes this business tick. In the box are the orthodoxies, the beliefs, and the shared mindset.

Orthodoxies are company specific. However, it is surprising how many company orthodoxies transcend a whole industry. Take the very old example of a supermarket: Even today, with all the advances in technology, I see in large supermarkets around the world a special cash register at the exit of the supermarket. It has a special sign and it says something like "Express: 7 items or less." Why do supermarkets offer the best service to their least valuable customers? What do they do for their most valuable customers?

Now, as a reader of this book you may want to check this in your local neighborhood, have you seen a till in a supermarket with a sign that reads something like "$300 or more…"? Please let me know immediately, because in all my global assignments I have not come across one. But then again I can immediately think about some interesting offers for those customers at the $300 or more till…

Dominant Logic – Dominant Hand

C. K. Prahalad understood the importance of a shared mindset in an organization. In 1986 he published on the concept of the dominant logic. This common/shared understanding provides the "glue" for an organization. People are attracted to join and to stay in an organization with a strong culture. However, when is the moment when changes in the environment create a turning point: When the positive glue turns into the negative blinkers?

Let us have a quick look, in Box 4.4, at the definitions of the key terms.

Dominant logic

Dominant logic is a mindset or a world view or conceptualization of the business and the administrative tools to accomplish goals and make decisions in that business. It is stored as a shared cognitive map (or set of schemas) among the dominant coalition. It is expressed as a learned, problem-solving behavior (Prahalad & Bettis, 1986).

Orthodoxy

Orthodoxy (from the Greek orthos ("right," "true," "straight")) and doxa ("opinion" or "belief," related to dokein, "to think"), is adherence to accepted norms. (Wikipedia)

Ideology

Ideology is a set of conscious and/or unconscious ideas that constitute one's goals, expectations, and actions. (Wikipedia) In business we have seen examples in the Toyota way or the Xerox way.

Shared Mindset

In decision theory and general systems theory, a mindset is a set of assumptions, methods, or notations held by one or more people or groups of people that is so established that it creates a powerful incentive within these people or groups to continue to adopt or accept prior behaviors, choices, or tools. This phenomenon is also sometimes described as mental inertia, "groupthink", or a "paradigm", and it is often difficult to counteract its effects upon analysis and decision making processes.

A mindset can also be seen as incident of a person's *Weltanschauung* or philosophy of life. (Wikipedia)

How do these concepts play out in practice? Sometimes in a very tangible manner. Recently I came to a new client to work with the CEO and the top team on the topic of innovation. The meeting took place in the headquarters of the organization. The very traditional building displayed the year 1836 as the founding year on the entrance. As I was ushered into the building, inevitably we had to go through the main hall, which was constructed like a dome. Dimmed lighting prevailed, but just enough to identify the paintings of the previous leaders. The founding fathers of the organization were even honored by bronze busts. The atmosphere immediately instills a sense of gravitas and responsibility. One thing was clear: During our innovation meeting with today's leaders the previous generations were literally looking over our shoulders. Surely, reinforcing the dominant hand of the organization…

The dominant logic may well be most visible in established organizations. However, much younger organizations also display the dominant logic, but maybe in a more subtle way. Therefore, the dominant logic is a precursor for the dominant hand at the organizational level.

Role of Values

From the dominant logic it is only a small step to get to the "values" of an organization. Many organizations, especially in the financial services industry, put "values" in the last few years at the top of their agenda. In these discussions the expected behaviors were clarified in terms of interacting with stakeholders as well with co-workers inside the organization.

Peter Drucker noted a long time ago that "people do not do what is expected, they do what is inspected." In terms of values, organizations usually have a clear list of expected behaviors. However, to what degree are these values actually inspected? Of course, the big-ticket items such as illegal or indecent behavior surely get well investigated and acted upon. It is less clear though when it comes to a value such as "collaboration." How do you know exactly when a co-worker has not collaborated? When and where is there a forum to address the potential value violation?

Leadership professor Dave Ulrich (1997) describes the managerial grid used at the time at General Electric (GE). At GE, Jack Welch introduced a matrix that brings two important aspects for performance management together. It offers the opportunity to link expectation to inspection.

Performance: Has an individual achieved the agreed performance targets in terms of sales, costs, budget, market share, and so on?

Values: Has an individual displayed behavior in accordance with the established values of the organization?

Clearly, as an organization you want co-workers to be fulfilling both performance criteria as well as displaying a behavior according to the values of the organization. It is also clear that individuals who are not fulfilling these criteria will not have much of a future in the organization.

Whilst the handling of these two quadrants is indeed straightforward, the real challenge is how to deal with individuals in the other two quadrants.

Take the top left-hand corner: Here we have an individual who is praised for behavior according to the values of the organization, but does not deliver on the agreed performance criteria. The recommended action is to identify and address the performance issue and offer support and development opportunities. Clearly, this person is being watched to ensure that indeed the performance picks up.

Now, finally the bottom right-hand corner: Here we find the high performers, the individuals who achieve, if not overachieve, on performance targets. However, they do that whilst in parallel not paying attention to the values of the organization. The example could be a sales person who is overachieving in her/his sales, but doing that at the expense of colleagues in a neighboring department. She/he may be violating the value of "collaboration." The recommended action here is to remind the person of the nature and the importance of values in the organization and insist on values being practiced. Also, this person is being watched closely.

Of course, all is fine when indeed the person is changing behavior to support the values of the organization. However, what should be done if this does not happen? Worse still, what if the individual continues to ignore the values and simultaneously continues to be the star performer according to sales figures or any other key performance indicator? This is the moment when large parts of the organization will be watching. This is the test for the importance of values. If the star performer is getting away with continuing the violation of values, the values will become meaningless in the organization.

There are two important challenges for leaders to apply this model:

1) Meeting performance targets next quarter.
2) Timing – when to proactively address the two dimensions.

Let us look at these two challenges in turn:

Performance targets

> "I cannot possibly lose my best performer! How do we meet our collective performance expectations next quarter/year?"

This is the most frequent argument I hear in discussions with senior leaders. Of course, these leaders have a point and it is indeed an important trade-off. However, over the years I have observed many leaders who took the easy way out and met the collective performance expectations – at the expense of the values propagated. In a short period of time this leads to a high degree of cynicism about values in the organization. People do what is inspected, not what is expected.

Timing

Official performance reviews in organizations are being conducted on the basis of the official performance review process. Now, this is done regularly, usually driven by the calendar year on a quarterly or annual basis. At these regular intervals feedback is provided based on the key performance indicators (KPIs) agreed. Now, this process works well for the dimension "performance," as sales figures and market share data can be clearly measured. What is much less clear is how to address the dimension "values." In a quarterly review process it is a little bit easier as the time horizon is much shorter than with an annual process. Therefore, both parties may have better memory of a value violation having taken place in say February. At the end of the year it is nearly impossible to have a meaningful discussion about what happened in February. What are the consequences? The discussion on values is being ticked-off; any real value violations may never get discussed.

The real challenge for leaders in applying this model is the issue of timing:

• Performance can be reviewed according to the calendar year.
• Values have to be enforced on a daily basis.

Here I have observed significant cultural differences. In organizations with an Anglo-Saxon heritage, this model is applied in a straightforward, no nonsense fashion. It is clearly communicated what the values are and any violations of these values will be addressed immediately as a backbone of a strong feedback culture.

However, in organizations influenced by a more consensus driven culture, this constitutes a huge challenge. Yes, we can measure performance in terms of targets achieved or not achieved. However, the other dimension, values, is proving to be the challenge. Are we clear about what these values are? Ok, we wrote something down at the last management away day, but is that for real? Does anyone remember? How can we measure them on a scale from one to ten?

In consensus driven cultures, such as in Germany, Switzerland, or Austria, organizations are struggling with this approach mightily. For values to be enforced, you cannot wait until the end of the quarter or even the end-of-year performance review, as you can do with the business performance dimension. This is daily business, this requires immediate intervention. Therefore, a strong feedback culture is very helpful here. In my observation this feedback culture is less developed in organizations from the more consensus driven cultures.

a strong feedback culture is very helpful

Based on a recent personal experience, I compare this challenge to training a puppy to become a proper member of the family household. What if, upon returning from three days of business travel, I was to summon the puppy for a performance review and explain that "on Monday you did something in the living room, on Tuesday you destroyed the sofa…"? The puppy's reaction would naturally be complete bewilderment; and this is why when training puppies an immediate intervention is warranted.

This is the analogy for enforcing values – it is hard daily business! So how can you actually do it?

In a well-documented corporate wide case (Bruch & Bieri, 2003), Hilti, the drilling machine manufacturer from Vaduz, Lichtenstein, has for years invested in their culture and its enforcement. With the mantra "love it, change it, leave it" they invite their co-workers to join in with a strong culture and liken it to playing soccer. However, when somebody walks on to the soccer pitch carrying a tennis racket, they are given a clear invitation to go back to the dressing room and return the racket. Alternatively, "change it" also implies finding enough tennis players inside Hilti to change the game altogether.

"Leave it" comes in two connotations:

1) Leave it for now – put the tennis racket to one side.
2) Realize that tennis is such a passion that you may be better suited to joining the neighboring tennis club than playing soccer with Hilti.

Now, the tennis racket scenario is a quite powerful metaphor for addressing value violations in a non-confrontational manner.

When Hanneke Frese after a successful career across Citibank became HR director at Zurich Financial Services quite a few years back, she introduced herself to her direct reports as follows:

> "My name is Hanneke, I am Dutch. In Holland we are used to talking in a clear language. I realize in Switzerland we have to be less direct. However, there are important values to me in our way of working together. Therefore, when I observe a value violation I reserve the right to raise my hand in the middle of a meeting and ask, 'Can we talk Dutch please?'"

With this very simple, but highly authentic and effective statement she had prepared the ground for being able to address value violations immediately, on a daily basis.

In numerous meetings and workshops I have tried to encourage individual leaders to develop their own, authentic metaphor for "Can we talk Dutch, please?" or to develop their own version of the tennis metaphor.

The implications for ambidexterity

As an architect for innovation, in your role as leader you have to create a culture for innovation, a culture to foster ambidexterity. Therefore, as part of the value system you have to clearly articulate that both exploitation and exploration are expected.

The challenge then in your leader role is how to embed that in the performance review system. How do you deal with individuals in the bottom right-hand corner of the matrix, the ones who have achieved their performance targets through exploitation, but have failed to engage in any exploration? Everyone in the organization will know who these individuals are, so it matters very much how these individuals are being led. If they are the ones who get the bonus and the promotion, the message is very clear to the rest of the organization. The need for exploration, the need for ambidexterity is on paper, in the strategic plans: But, when it comes to the crunch, delivering results next quarter through exploitation is what really matters.

The consequences are quite dramatic: Everyone in the organization understands that the need for exploration is rather hollow. Why would anyone risk his/her career for exploration projects?

In your role as architect for ambidexterity you should ensure that it is not just expected but also inspected.

Mindset Challenge – Structural Ambidexterity as a Last Resort

In terms of processes for ambidexterity we have already, in Chapter 1, looked at the two strategic options for how an organization can address opportunities. Option one is choosing the structural approach, to structurally separate the processes of ambidexterity. There is one organizational set-up, a single structure and performance scorecard for "exploitation", running and developing the core business. Exploration would then take place in a unit structurally separate from the exploitation efforts. Again, the exploration unit would have their own structure, processes, and performance scorecards.

Option two is addressing the ambidexterity opportunity contextually. This means that both exploration and exploitation take place within the same structural unit. The unit leader has to decide in which "context," the exploitation or exploration innovation activity takes place. Depending on that context the leader would differentiate the approach both in the process required and the scorecards applied.

Now, this choice between structural or contextual ambidexterity could be viewed as a strategic organizational choice. However, I have chosen to discuss it in Chapter 4 Mindset Challenges. In the last few years I have encountered too many discussions with leaders in organizations around this topic, which usually start with "Everyone knows…" or "We believe…" So it is worth investigating a little bit deeper what is behind these beliefs around how to best organize for ambidexterity.

It is not a surprise, that the research into ambidexterity at the organizational level has established that the choice of "contextual ambidexterity" is more successful than the structural approach. Why is this so obvious?

"contextual ambidexterity is more successful than the structural approach"

Let us work this through. In contextual ambidexterity, the logic goes hand in hand with the research which established that "leadership at all levels" is superior compared to looking at management for junior levels, reserving leadership for the top echelons of the organization. Let us revisit what the roles of managers and leaders are:

- Managers implement clear targets and enforce implementation – they do things right.
- Leaders do the right things.

Now, the right things can be identified at various levels of the hierarchy. Organizations that create an environment for exploration also at the junior levels are likely to create a culture driven by alertness – being awake and responsive. When experimentation and exploration can also take place at the lower ranks of the hierarchy, the culture will embrace openness to change and in fact there should be no shortage of talent already well versed in both exploitation and exploration activities.

However, by separating exploration and exploitation in different structural settings it can be expected that a different level of alertness is on display. The exploitation folk will pride themselves on running the engine that lets the organization steam forward. They are quite likely to look down on their exploration colleagues, as the people who live in dreamland and who are spending the scarce resources so painfully earned in the main business. Likewise, the exploration folk will look at the exploitation people as being "so last century." The patterns described above were quite clearly displayed in the last 20 years in telephone companies around the globe. The traditional fixed-line businesses, with their entrenched customer base and their well-proven business models, versus the mobile phone folk, with their hip, future-oriented approach.

The big challenge for the organization is indeed the consolidation of exploitation and exploration activities. Now, investors and shareholders may be the first to pick this up. They will very quickly ask the right questions:

What is the value to shareholders of having both units under one roof?

Do we not create more shareholder value by spinning off one of the two businesses?

These are indeed strong arguments so that the organization's management team will have to demonstrate the synergies between the businesses. Therefore, they will force the two structural units to demonstrate tangible synergetic projects.

This is exactly where the crunch for the top team is: If they let two separate units run in their own independent ways, how likely is it really that the main organization is embracing a new concept developed by the exploration team? Not very likely at all. The not invented here syndrome will prove to be a tough challenge that has been delegated upwards to the top team for resolution. This situation reinforces the view that indeed the top team does leadership; the rest of the organization is doing management. This flies in the face of the leadership research which makes a very compelling case for leadership at all levels and points out that leaders and managers are not two different people, but two different roles.

So, if the logic is so compelling to go with the contextual approach, why can we observe in so many organizations the structural approach, separating exploitation and exploration? It is the only way for them to do it! History in many organizations has demonstrated that many existing leaders find it extremely challenging to demonstrate proactively ambidextrous behavior. If in doubt and under pressure they revert back to exploitation: Therefore, playing safe for themselves and the organization. The gains are very much short term; the focus is on numbers for the next quarter or this year. However, this is exactly the behavior that can lead organizations only to focus on the existing business and miss out on the next phase in the industry's development.

I have spoken to many CEOs and senior executives from a number of industries about this puzzle, of the appearance of two separate units. In their responses, the pride they feel in having set up a separate unit to do the "beyond" innovation is immediately obvious. The argument is that this sends a positive message to the investor community:

> "Yes, we are addressing the future while simultaneously not neglecting the core business."
>
> "However, we want the exploration guys to do the free thinking, without being hampered by old thinking."
>
> "In our company we want clear focus; both groups have this clear focus."

Then, privately and off the record these senior executives admit that the separation of exploitation and exploration is only moving the tension upwards, it does not take the generic pressure of ambidexterity away. Instead of the strain being felt by the individual leaders across the whole organization, these leaders have very smartly delegated the topic back to senior management. At this point the top management team has to deal with the tension. The "monkey" is on the back of the top team, some of whom may actually enjoy the extra importance and the extra levers for decision making.

Meanwhile, the senior executives in the core business focus on polishing the existing business. They can take great pride in the fact that they are contributing the most to the overall performance of the organization.

When they are then successfully focusing on the current business they also have a very good excuse for not exploring anymore: "Top management has just set up this separate team, so let us see what these smart people can do..." At this stage the senior executives have just abdicated from any responsibility for exploration. There is a great opportunity to just hide for a while to focus on making the numbers in their exploitation arena. The people in these positions are often very seasoned warriors for the organization. They may have seen a number of CEOs come and go. Certainly they will have seen numerous top managers come and go. They will play it safe. They will not get engaged in any risky exploration activities, this is the Teflon approach and is where the *Lehmschicht*, the layer of clay, sets in.

So, now let us look at the people in the "beyond" units. These units are set up with a purpose because top management gets increasingly nervous about ambidexterity in the organization and watching the assigned leaders always revert back to exploitation. At some point they will call consultants in to look at the organization's innovation portfolio. The result may be alarming – too many projects in exploitation, not enough in exploration.

Now, the CEO's gut feeling is confirmed that in the current organizational structure exploration is not possible. What do other companies do? Yes, they set up separate units to do "beyond" innovation, and yes in order to succeed they get a direct line to the CEO.

Ok, the structural decision is made: a beyond unit will be set up. Where will the people come from? Certainly not from inside, the insiders had their chance and have not taken it. So outsiders are brought in to introduce fresh ideas. Then the realization hits that the entire team cannot be made up of outsiders, a respected seasoned organizational insider is needed for balance and to keep contact with the core business.

After a while the beyond team is in place, reporting as closely as possible directly to the CEO, maybe with a seasoned hand in between. So let us play this out: There are now two structural units responsible for innovation. The first unit is in charge of innovation around the core business, with a clear focus on exploitation, using the existing structural responsibilities. In parallel the beyond unit is newly installed with a direct link to the CEO. What is the relationship going to look like when both set-ups are fully operational?

Not friendly, to put it mildly. The exploitation camp will look at the beyond team as having no idea about business realities in this industry. The beyond people will look at the exploitation unit as the defenders of the past. Will these two structural units collaborate? Not naturally, though maybe upon the specific request of the CEO and/or the top management team.

In the organizational set-up just described, where is the organizational conflict being resolved? Yes, at the top team level!

What are the implications for the rest of the organization? The majority of employees will feel compelled to focus on the core business, leaving any rational and emotional responsibility for exploration to the beyond team – and the top management team. The practical effect is that the majority of the organization is in no way engaged to explore anything beyond the core business.

Profile of members of the beyond team – intrapreneur vs entrepreneur

So, how do the members of the beyond team react? Initially they react with a great level of enthusiasm. They have the ear of the CEO who will be eager to show some early success. The newly recruited entrepreneurs – not intrapreneurs! – will enjoy the comfort of the corporate budgets compared to the typical resources in a frugal start-up situation. So they now have the budgets, the positional power of the CEO, and their already well established outside networking contacts – what can stop them? Success – in the launch of a new beyond business, for example. Yes, it has been launched but the regulatory arrangements may not allow for the business to be owned by the organization. Therefore, the new business has to be sold to an organization that does not have the same regulatory boundaries. Even if any regulatory hurdles can be taken, the new business may indeed cannibalize the existing business and come under intense "friendly fire" from the rest of the organization.

Here is where the distinction of intrapreneurs and entrepreneurs comes in again. Entrepreneurs after a while are quite likely to leave the beyond team in frustration of the organizational constraints. It is the intrapreneurs who will have the patience and stamina to see the projects through inside the organization. Now, the entrepreneurs when exiting are not necessarily worse off. If the new business concept is spun-off by the organization, they may choose to stay with the concept in the new environment. Leaving the organization may in fact lead to a whole new set of opportunities based on the experience gained.

The choice between structural and contextual ambidexterity is very much driven by the dominant logic in the organization and the beliefs of the members of the top team. Both options have significant implementation challenges from a leadership perspective.

Learning Organization vs Forgetting Organization

Organizations have their dominant logic, history, and DNA code. If the organization embraces the concept of ambidexterity, it will require change. Therefore, it is important to have a quick look at some valuable concepts from the change perspective.

The iceberg analogy may explain the importance of the DNA code of an organization. Above the water surface you see the products, services, and structures of an organization: Below the surface you have the culture, shared mindset, and orthodoxies. It is very quickly possible to change the part above the surface; it takes much longer to change the issues below the surface (see the example in Box 4.5).

BOX 4.5 FINANCIAL SERVICES EXAMPLE

At a global financial services workshop we exchanged best practice experiences around innovation and change. As people took turns in showcasing their experiences, we then had a presentation from an organization that had grown by acquisition. The presenter explained: "It is our strategy to grow by acquisition and we have done that quite successfully during the previous few years. Part of our strategy is to do the merger integration at Easter." The other participants looked at him in bewilderment and then somebody asked the obvious question: "What has merger integration got to do with a religious holiday?" The answer came promptly. "It is key to the integration with our newly acquired organization that we get our IT systems organized. At Easter we have four days, Friday to Monday, as bank holidays. This gives us the window to complete the merger integration without disturbing our customers."

The example in Box 4.5 demonstrates that you can change the structure and processes in an organization very rapidly. However, this is the part above the water surface in the iceberg model, the rational side. The part below the water surface, the emotional part, cannot be integrated in four days.

Learning

A lot of attention has been given to how organizations learn. Starting with the work at Boston Consulting Group (BCG) in the 1960s, the focus was very much based on the "experience curve." The conclusions, initially based on analyzing aircraft manufacturers, were that there is a positive correlation between the number of units produced of a certain model and the cost incurred. Now, that is in itself not so surprising as this focuses on continued improvement, benchmarking – in the language of ambidexterity, on exploitation.

Then in the late 1980s and the 1990s Peter Senge (1990) and his colleagues developed the concept of the "learning organization." They focused on five main features:

1) Systems thinking.
2) Personal mastery.
3) Mental models.
4) Shared vision.
5) Team learning.

This concept then encouraged many organizations to act much more holistically across the organization. In particular experts in learning &

development and organizational development focused their work on linking the learning at the individual level to the learning at the organizational level.

What does that mean for ambidexterity? Yes, learning is critical for the exploitation part. Benchmarking, knowledge transfer, and best practices are all very important activities that encourage organizations to deliver on exploitation activities. But what about the exploration part?

Forgetting

> Executives must also remember to focus the organization on the "forgetting curve." They must identify the behaviors, practices, and beliefs that are increasingly becoming dysfunctional or counterproductive and put in place ways of discarding them. Indeed, during a corporate transformation, the forgetting curve is sometimes more important than the learning curve.
>
> C. K. Prahalad (2010)

Summary

In this chapter we have looked at the soft factors in organizations and how these impact the ability to create ambidextrous businesses. After some 30 years of working with organizations on innovation and change, I view the "mindset challenges" as the toughest. Organizations with strong cultures and a history of success have created a deep sense of how business is done there. They have created a strong identity, which keeps the organization powering along, very much supporting the exploitation arm of ambidexterity.

In successful organizations and industries it is very common that strong dominant mindsets emerge. The question is: When do these dominant mindsets become blinkers? These blinkers may then allow new competitors to come in. Even the car industry has been very surprised by the recent success of start-up Tesla. As this book is being written, ever new applications for 3-D printers

When do these dominant mindsets become blinkers?

are being developed, challenging the assumptions and mindsets in many industries.

Orthodoxies

In normal business situations orthodoxies are always present. However, nobody ever talks about them. It is only in special workshop sessions that these orthodoxies can be specifically addressed. Initially met with bewilderment, executives quickly engage in the process of identifying orthodoxies. Within a few minutes the orthodoxies are identified. Then the big surprise is when comparing their insights to what colleagues have identified before – it is usually very similar. Therefore, orthodoxies seem to transcend different businesses and geographies in one organization. However, core orthodoxies also transcend companies in the same industry.

What are the consequences? Orthodoxies are like a magnet pulling the organization back to its core. From an ambidexterity perspective, orthodoxies pull organizations to innovate in exploitation mode. Orthodoxies, however, will work like antibodies to fight exploration projects.

For any exploration project to succeed there has to be a mechanism to deal with the orthodoxies. They will be there, the question is how can you identify them and find robust ways of addressing them.

Orthodoxies can be a source for idea generation. This sounds contradictory at first, as exploration projects will be fought by the orthodoxies. That may be the case, but when you take an orthodoxy and turn it on its head, then a whole new set of ideas will emerge.

Take the example of the supermarket "Express: 7 items or less" cash register. Instead of offering the best service to the least valuable customer, how about offering something different to the most valuable customer? Maybe offering a special counter for spends of $300 or more. Here we are probably dealing with a family purchase, so special services could be offered, such as helping to take the groceries to the car.

The role of values

On the positive side, the power of the dominant logic in an organization provides the glue that holds the organization together. It is in effect a key part of the organizational culture. Now, organizational cultures are also supported by explicit organizational values. In recent years many organizations have put significant efforts into documenting their values and making them transparent to all co-workers. The big challenge is, in many cases, how to enforce the values documented. As Peter Drucker famously said: People do not do what is expected, they do what is inspected.

The value performance matrix brings together two key dimensions for the individual performance review:

- How well has the individual co-worker performed against the key performance indicators, such as sales, cost, and so on?
- How well did the co-worker perform against the values?

The challenge for leaders is that performance can be reviewed according to regular calendar intervals, quarterly, or annually, but values have to be enforced daily.

Why do values matter in ambidexterity? When an ambidextrous organization expects their leaders to value both exploitation and exploration it in fact becomes a value. This poses the challenge: Do organizations also inspect? In order to build an ambidextrous organization symbols matter:

- What happens to the individual who is a star performer in exploitation, but provides no input to exploration? Promotion?
- What happens to the individual who recommended killing an exploration project? Promotion?

If ambidexterity is being placed on the organization's agenda everyone will be watching what happens to the individuals who either do exploitation only or who dare to take on a risky exploration project. Symbols matter…

This chapter has discussed also the case for using contextual rather than structural ambidexterity. I have a high level of sympathy for top teams in organizations who decide to set up separate exploration units for "beyond innovation" as far away as possible from innovation in the core business. These organizations and their top teams may have become disillusioned with the way their senior executives have dealt with ambidexterity before. Especially when they observe that at the senior management level everyone is quickly resorting back to the presumably safe heavens of the core market. The CEO should rightly be worried about the lack of attention to exploration as it is providing a great opportunity for new entrants to shape the next phase of the industry. So what is the natural outcome? To create a new unit and have it report as closely as possible to the CEO.

With this decision the CEO and the top team may have just created a significant challenge for the organization:

• There are the core business teams.
• There are the "beyond" teams.

It is very unlikely that the two camps will collaborate. In addition comes the outside pressure. Investors and analysts have been informed and will start putting pressure on the top team. Senior management is now under observation from the investors and the analysts: Indeed, the whole organization is watching how the top team is implementing ambidexterity.

The core business people can wash their hands and can declare, "We only focus on the core business. Let the top team and – the often new – exploration guys sort out the new stuff." They and their organizations will retreat into two modes:

1) We do as we are told.
2) Managers not leaders.

The implications are significant; the culture has potentially shifted from leaders at all levels to a managers and leaders hierarchy.

Mindset challenges – What is the impact for you?

In your role as manager you have to understand the current dominant logic and the associated mindset. In order to do things "right" you have to function and operate within the current mindset.

In your role as leader you have to challenge the status quo, and the mindset, to identify the behaviors, practices, and beliefs that are increasingly becoming dysfunctional or counterproductive and put in place ways of discarding them.

In your role as architect:

- Try to get the contextual approach to ambidexterity going.
- Proactively engage your leadership team in identifying orthodoxies in your business and develop explicit ways of addressing these orthodoxies.
- Take care how the individuals in exploration projects are treated, especially when recommending killing the project. Symbols matter…

In your role as project leader:

- Watch out for proper sponsorship, this is now getting very political!
- Be clear about which orthodoxies your project is challenging and develop robust responses.
- Use orthodoxies as a source for idea generation. Turn the orthodoxy on its head: What would we do if this orthodoxy did not exist? For example, in the supermarket: 7 items or less vs $300 or more.

Finally, mindset challenges are the toughest challenges in building the ambidextrous organization. This is why it is addressed in this final chapter of Part I, as the pinnacle of the challenges identified. Mindset challenges are always based on emotional elements, transcending the clear rational elements we often associate with running an organization.

Ambidextrous organizations are not start-up organizations. Ambidextrous organizations have a history, a track record. Going forward it seems to be prudent to explicitly pay attention to the shared mindset developed and to honor the past successes. However, let me finish with a quote:

> Indeed, during a corporate transformation, the forgetting curve is sometimes more important than the learning curve.
>
> C. K. Prahalad (2010)

Summary: Part I

The first part of the book has attempted to identify and structure the challenges for building ambidextrous organizations from both an individual and an organizational perspective.

Awareness of the Topic

Ambidexterity calls for exploring the new while exploiting the now. Therefore this first part of this book aimed at addressing the challenges for simultaneously exploring and exploiting.

As we all observe signs of the convergence of industries around us, the Google Car, Nespresso, Senseo, wristbands, etc., the reaction of both individual leaders and organizations is hesitant. Yes, there are some organizations that proactively and collectively address the opportunities and yes there are individual opinion leaders in organizations who enthusiastically address the opportunities and threats associated. However, Part I has identified the need to address the challenges of ambidexterity comprehensively, at both the individual and the organizational level. Changes in the external environment such as an aging population will only increase the need to build ambidextrous organizations.

Why is it Important?

To address the topic of ambidexterity is important from two perspectives.

From a defensive perspective, as a leader in your industry you may have to focus on exploitation in order to deliver quarter after quarter on sales, market share, and profit targets. However, exploitation will focus you on the existing market and you will be dependent on the future relevance of that market. It will not help you much to be the market leader in the typewriter business...

However, convergence of industries is offering great opportunities for shaping new markets. In recent years we have seen the emergence of whole new industries such as smartphones and tablets. How can you explore new opportunities beyond your current industry, shaping new markets and possibly new industries?

Organizational Structure

How an organization addresses ambidexterity is a strategic choice. A company can choose to run exploitation within one unit, for instance in an R&D team, as well as in the dedicated exploration group. The other option is to choose "contextual ambidexterity," implying that individual leaders are charged with both exploitation and exploration simultaneously. This structural ambidexterity describes the deliberate separation of exploitation and exploration processes. All the evidence from academic research seems to favor the solution of contextual ambidexterity. The advantage being that the consolidation and imple- mentation of new ideas can be achieved at the appropriate level in the organization.

The choice around organizational structure is as much a strategic decision as it is a "mindset" decision, based on what seems to work best for your organization.

Organizational Processes

For organizations opting for the structural ambidexterity route it is fairly straightforward. The leaders in the exploitation and exploration units will implement the most appropriate processes and performance management systems. These will be quite different from each other. Most organizations that opt for the contextual solution are more challenged. The "innovation funnel" – the usually well-established collection of processes around exploitation – is then equally used for exploration processes. The key challenge for ambidextrous leaders is to realize that exploitation and exploration require different processes. The key difference is the notion of "failure" – a "kill" recommendation by the project leader of an exploration project should not be considered failure.

Leader/Manager

Throughout this book the importance of individuals in shaping an organization is addressed. The concept of the two roles for individuals as managers and leaders is paramount. The leadership research demonstrates that leadership at all levels is the hallmark of successful organizations. The concept of leaders and managers implies that it is not dependent on hierarchy but that it is driven by two different roles an individual can take in an executive function.

In the context of ambidexterity, the notion of "exploitation" is very much associated with an individual taking on the role as a manager. Exploration explicitly calls for individuals accepting their role as leader.

Forum

Ambidexterity creates numerous challenges at both the individual and the organizational level. The question is where and when can these challenges be discussed? What is the right forum? Is it the boardroom? Is it the annual top 80 conference? Should it be part of the strategic planning process? Could it form an explicit part of the learning and development curriculum?

Mindset/Dominant Logic

As individuals and as organizations we have our unique DNA code, the experiences over the years that show us how to be successful and what to avoid. As we move purposefully into ambidexterity as individuals and organizations we become exposed to these orthodoxies. They will have two different forms of impact. They may pull us back, to abandon exploration and steer us back into the presumably safe waters of exploitation. Or, the purposeful challenging of orthodoxies, may offer us a key to opening up new opportunities. What would happen if in a supermarket we had a till with a "$300 or more" sign? What would happen if in financial services we dealt with customers with the highest risk?

Part II
Solutions

Introduction to Part II

The Role of Individual and Organizational Bandwidth

This book addresses the building of ambidextrous organizations from both an individual and an organizational perspective. Two organizational processes have already been identified in Part I as key drivers for building ambidextrous organizations:

- Corporate development (strategy).
- Individual development (leadership development).

In Part II we will address the key ingredients for building ambidextrous organizations.

The Structure of Part II

Chapter 5 looks at possible approaches in linking aspects of development – corporate and individual development. Chapter 6 looks at the solutions provided by external scouting activities. Chapter 7 lays out the role of purposeful engineering in creating appropriate partnerships.

Chapter 8 discusses approaches to managing risk. That is, how to derisk the exposure inherent in ambidexterity for both the organization and the individual.

In this introduction to Part II I will discuss the logic for the solutions identified. In the first section the baseline for the solution space will be established. Data points will be taken from the Fall of 2014, summarizing insights from strategists and experts in leadership development. Based on these insights the concept of "bandwidth" will be introduced. This is how both individuals and organizations can develop their competencies and capabilities to use both hands.

The Baseline Fall of 2014: Summarizing Insights from Strategists and Development Experts

This book was written in the Fall of 2014. In order to anchor the recommendations based on the most recent insights, the following data sources are used:

- McKinsey September 2014 Forum of Business School Professors and Corporates.
- EFMD Forum of Business Schools and L&D Professionals, October 2014.

In the McKinsey Forum, scholars and practitioners discussed the current status of strategy research and its application in business in general. They came up with a seven-point plan for help (McKinsey Quarterly 2014).

The seven needs identified by workshop participants for today's strategist consist of the following:

1) Techniques for identifying structural versus cyclical changes in the external environment.

2) Techniques for spotting and harnessing cross-functional capabilities that a company has and may be able to leverage for competitive advantage.
3) Tools for stimulating the creation of options, particularly where change is occurring rapidly and the scope for strategic action is shifting.
4) Tools for stimulating the understanding of forces that are truly dynamic, with multiple second-, third-, and fourth-order effects.
5) Proven tools for improving strategy processes, breaking inertia, and jolting conventional thinking.
6) Techniques for generating and harnessing insights from big data about customers, competitors, and suppliers.
7) Techniques for identifying and focusing the top team's attention on new or poorly understood risks – before it is too late.

What is interesting here is the strategists' need for tools and techniques. Now, in this list not much differentiation is being made between the organization, the strategy unit, or the individual in charge of strategy development. When related to ambidexterity, the topics identified in these seven points touch on many of the issues which have already been covered in Part I, where the challenges for ambidexterity were identified and discussed in detail.

The EFMD Conference in October 2014 explicitly looked at the topic of ambidexterity from a leadership and development perspective (Figure I.II.1).

The learning and development (L&D) experts thought that a lot of potential exists in bringing their expertise to the table, especially beyond the existing processes. As can be seen from Figures I.II.1 and I.II.2, the highest potential was seen in using L&D expertise when it comes to concrete business development initiatives. However, that was narrowly followed by the potential to align internal business development processes with outside partners.

Given the situation that we have at our fingertips the insights of key strategists and key L&D experts, Part II can then focus on solutions for building ambidextrous organizations.

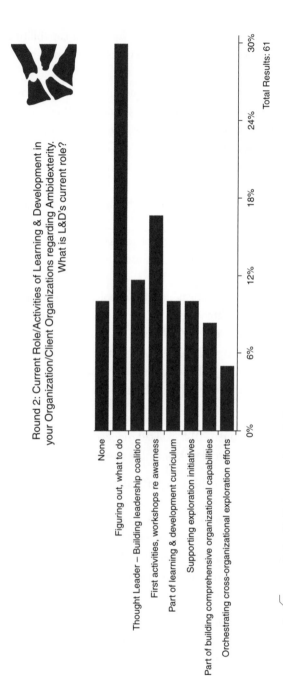

Round 2: Current Role/Activities of Learning & Development in your Organization/Client Organizations regarding Ambidexterity. What is L&D's current role?

Total Results: 61

FIGURE I.II.1 Current Role of L&D Experts in Ambidexterity

Source: Maier, J. EFMD conference keynote speech, St. Gallen, October 2, 2014.

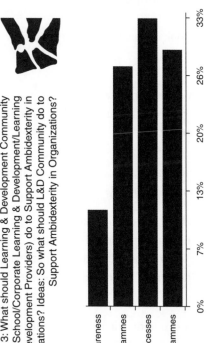

Round 3: What should Learning & Development Community (Business School/Corporate Learning & Development/Learning and Development Providers) do to Support Ambidexterity in Organizations? Ideas: So what should L&D Community do to Support Ambidexterity in Organizations?

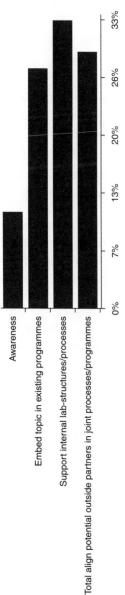

FIGURE 1.II.2 What Should the Learning and Development Community do to Support Ambidexterity in Organizations?

Source: Maier, J. EFMD conference keynote speech, St. Gallen, October 2, 2014.

Increasing the "Bandwidth" of Individual Competencies and Organizational Capabilities

Ambidexterity as discussed in this book requires development at two levels:

1) Individual – can we build the individual's competencies?
2) Organizational – can we build the right capabilities, including the right robust processes to handle ambidexterity?

What it amounts to is an increase in the bandwidth of individual competence and the bandwidth of organizational capability.

In terms of ambidexterity both individuals and organizations have a preference for behavior. In the case of individuals it is best described as "personality." For organizations it is more likely to be called culture/dominant logic. In both cases it relates to the "dominant" hand and the capacity to develop the use of "both hands."

Now, as a starting point it is important to understand for both individuals and organizations what this preference for behavior actually is. This understanding is important because under pressure both individuals and organizations will quite easily take shelter in their comfort zone; which means they will retract to their preference for behavior.

Ambidexterity means to be able to use both hands equally well. Therefore, both ambidextrous individuals and ambidextrous organizations have to address the challenge of bandwidth. This means how far away from their natural preference for behavior can they move without losing authenticity. Bandwidth then describes the spectrum on a scale between zero and 100 that an individual or an organization can cover for a given preference for behavior.

Let us look at two examples. One addresses the individual leader; the other focuses on the organization.

Individual Leader

As addressed in Chapter 2, the personality of individual leaders matters. We introduced the big five (neuroticism, extraversion, openness to change, agreeableness, and conscientiousness), as a concept to illustrate that preference for behavior in individuals is quite stable after the teenage years. We also used the T-Model to illustrate how leaders over time develop their own leadership style. We identified adaptability and authenticity as key drivers for successful leaders.

Adaptability is the key to understanding the importance of bandwidth. For instance, if on a scale from zero to 100 your score on extraversion is 85 you can be considered to have a preference for extraverted behavior. In addition, you may also score 90 on conscientiousness. Now, this combination of preferences for behavior on both extraversion and conscientiousness may well support you in your early career as you will gain visibility and your leader-like behavior may persuade other people to follow you. As a result, you may achieve good results in your functional area of responsibility. You have created a good track record and possibly even a great reputation in exploitation.

Now, as you are also challenged to lead exploration projects you have to influence partners from different parts of your own organization and possibly from other organizations. You may have to play down your high score on extraversion; otherwise the partners may feel steamrolled. How far can you push it down? Your actual score on extraversion will remain at 85, but how will the other partners view you? Can they see you as 65, 45, or 30? There is a difference in the bandwidth whether you can cover a range of 85 to 65 or whether you can manage even 85–30. In the first case the bandwidth covers 85 – 65 = 20 points, in the latter case it covers 85 – 30 = 55 points.

As a second example, an individual who scores 27 on extraversion, indicating that he/she is indeed quite introverted, has to convince a network of partners to follow an exciting business opportunity. Here it matters whether the network partners see him/her as 27, 50, or even 80. To be seen as being enthusiastic about the business opportunity will clearly help. Therefore, it matters whether the person can muster a bandwidth of 60 – 27 = 33 points or 80 – 27 = 53 points.

The bandwidth provides an indication, a measure for the degree of adaptability an individual can muster. The higher the bandwidth is, the higher the level of adaptability.

Developing a higher level of bandwidth

Analysis should be the starting point. Where are you located on a scale from zero to 100 on the big five or any other personality model? This will provide the anchor point. Then, as the second part of the analysis, it matters what the context is, it matters what the expectations are of recipients, the audience, and the partners. Understanding the anchor point and the expectation points will indicate the bandwidth the individual has to cover.

Now, for individuals doing this analysis for the first time, the results may turn out to be quite daunting. They may realize that the bandwidth they need to cover may well be way outside their comfort zone. So, how can individuals increase their own bandwidth? How can they move from 27 in extraversion to a perceived of 80? It goes back to the analogy introduced in the Introduction, signing your name. Your personal signature you will always conduct with your dominant hand. However, in the case of a skiing accident, breaking your dominant hand, you will have to learn to use the other hand for a certain period of time. At first it will feel very uncomfortable when putting the pen in the other hand. However, I am sure that by the time your dominant hand has recovered from the skiing accident you will be quite capable in using the other hand. What it requires is patience and a lot of practice.

The same is true for the individual leader realizing that she/he may have to develop the other hand in order to increase the bandwidth of her/his leadership repertoire. It requires practice for an extraverted person to hold back in meetings, to purposefully listen to other people. It requires practice for an introverted person to purposefully express the passion required to win the hearts and minds of network partners to follow in an exploration project. And it will take time and practice for a person scoring high on conscientiousness to deal with uncertainty and ambiguity in an exploration project.

The outcome is that the more an individual leader can increase his/her bandwidth in leadership behavior, the more adaptable they will become. For individual leaders, adaptability is often the most difficult challenge. However, it is not the only challenge, as followers also expect authenticity. As leaders try to extend their bandwidth, their leadership repertoire, followers will immediately check for how genuine this new, unexpected behavior is. They will spot "acting" – so leaders must be genuinely convinced by their own story and consistently stick to it.

Organizational Bandwidth

To get an understanding of the challenges faced by an organization it is a good starting point to look at the innovation landscape for an organization as discussed in Chapter 1. With the ten types of innovation we looked at:

- Business model; how do we get paid?
- Networking; inside and outside the industry.
- Enabling process.
- Core process.
- Product performance.
- Service.
- Product system.
- Channel.
- Brand.
- Customer experience.

How does this relate to the bandwidth of an organization? In the middle of this model you have:

- Product performance.
- Product.
- Service.

Organizations focusing on these three areas for innovation will have identified the function of research and development (R&D) teams as key drivers for innovation. Organizations that include channel, brand and customer experience will also have identified sales/marketing as key drivers for innovation.

Organizations which identify innovation in areas such as core processes and enabling processes will cast the net for innovation wider still. They would include "process owners" in those responsible for innovation within a company. These process owners would cover functional areas such as manufacturing, supply chain management, and compliance as driver for innovation.

Networking innovation looks at the potential in partnering with other organizations, both inside and outside the industry. Partnering can come in different guises, ranging from mere collaboration to joint ventures and full-blown takeovers. In this sphere the responsibilities for innovation include functional areas such as mergers and acquisitions (M&A) and legal.

Business model innovation, defined here as "how do we get paid?" clearly involves the expertise of key players in the finance department.

Bandwidth in organizations

Over the years I have come across different bandwidths for innovation.

R&D focus

In many technology driven organizations and R&D led industries I have observed a clear R&D focus. The implications are twofold:

1) R&D feels very powerful and confident to be the main driver of the organization's future.
2) Other functional departments abdicate any responsibility for innovation and let the R&D folks get on with it.

As a consequence, the organizational bandwidth for innovation is very narrow. That means the responsibility for innovation is not shared across the organization.

As witnessed in a recent innovation workshop with an R&D team realization can come very fast:

- Do we know anyone in marketing?
- How do we get supply chain management involved?
- How do our competitors do it?

As these R&D experts were sweating over how to expand innovation beyond R&D, their colleagues in other departments were quite merrily fulfilling their own performance agreements. However, these performance agreements usually do not extend into the notion of innovation.

As an outsider coming into such an environment you can immediately smell danger. The danger lies in the strong possibility that any innovation in the organization will be of an exploitation nature, with no platform for purposeful "exploration" at the same time.

Joint R&D and marketing workshops – increasing the bandwidth

Organizations with a strong R&D culture as a source for innovation, often as a next step in their organizational development, focus on joint meetings between the experts in technology and the experts in sales and marketing. This means that they are getting closer to their promise of delivering superb customer experience to their clients.

The low hanging fruits here are in avoiding any delays to getting new products and services out as quickly as possible to their customers.

Commercialization is the buzzword that then unites the R&D and sales and marketing teams.

This approach significantly broadens the bandwidth of the organization. However, it broadens the bandwidth in a way that strengthens the exploitation side of ambidexterity. The logic is that by better collaboration between R&D and sales and marketing the new products will reach the organization's customers earlier in a well-coordinated fashion. In fact, it makes the organization more efficient.

Now, how can we make the organization more effective? How can we move beyond R&D and sales and marketing? How can we include other key processes such as manufacturing, supply chain management, and possibly the financial experts who may have key insights and experience in terms of financial engineering?

So, the question is: What can be a possible forum to explicitly address the opportunities across the organizational bandwidth? There are three potential categories:

CEO conference: The annual gathering of the top executives (top 50, top 100; senior management conference, etc.). At this conference all key functions are represented and the organizational bandwidth is at its maximum potential. However, this forum is rarely used to launch exploration projects. The forum is usually used to create an overall strategic alignment to strategic and financial objectives as well as ensuring that through social events, the top executives can better function as members of a top team.

Special task force: The top management team may decide to set up a special task force to purposefully address exploration opportunities requiring the maximum organizational bandwidth. However, this method oftentimes involves the assignment of an outside consulting group. If this happens, the ownership of the process is transferred to outside partners.

Top talent development program: As the organization is identifying and developing the future leaders, top talent from across the organization are brought together. Therefore, by default, a cohort of 30 or 40 top talent will mirror key functions and markets. Indeed, this is a forum which by definition displays a very high degree of organizational bandwidth.

Increasing the Bandwidth for Both Individuals and Organizations

Strategy experts identified a strong need for tools and techniques in the McKinsey Forum in the Fall of 2014. The L&D experts at the EFMD Conference in the Fall of 2014 identified the need for better-connected processes between L&D and organizational/strategy development.

Increasing the bandwidth of both the individual and the organization is the key challenge regarding ambidexterity. In Part II of this book potential solutions will be discussed.

chapter 5

Solution – Linking Leadership Development to Corporate Development

Why is this Important for You and for Your Organization?

In this book we discuss ambidexterity from two perspectives, the individual leader and the organization. In the introduction to Part II we discussed the development opportunities for both individuals and organizations in order to increase their respective "bandwidth." In this chapter we will investigate approaches to purposefully linking individual development opportunities to organizational development.

From your individual perspective, you will get inspiration on how to purposefully use exploration opportunities in your organization to foster your personal development. From an organizational perspective you may take away insights on how to link two organizational processes: Leadership development and strategy development.

Many large organizations in recent years have established their own corporate universities with the purpose of creating organization-specific development opportunities. I will discuss this specific situation in the light of ambidexterity and will offer insights on how the link between the strategic agenda and the key people in an organization can be managed.

The Arena for Linking Leadership Development to Corporate Development

As we develop solutions towards building ambidextrous organizations it is worth looking at the linkages between increasing the bandwidth of the individual leader and increasing the bandwidth of the organization. Figure 5.1, demonstrates these inter-linkages between leadership development and corporate development. This chart was developed over the years and was very much influenced by Professor Gordon Hewitt's (2013) initial input.

This framework brings together the interaction of relevant organizational processes related to ambidexterity:

Leadership development: The purposeful development of individual's competencies.

Strategy development: The organization's strategic process for determining the choices made from the strategic option space.

Capability development: The organization's response to collectively addressing opportunities and challenges through developing robust processes.

Exploration initiatives: Concrete exploration projects addressing specific opportunities identified.

In this framework (Figure 5.1) it is obvious that it does not matter from where you start to address ambidexterity. Let us look at possible options.

Option 1

We start with the logic of individual leadership development and make it part of the leadership curriculum. Participants will immediately want to see the strategic relevance to their organization and the encouragement from top management and/or strategy development or business development. From this, it is a small step to launch exploration projects, bringing us from step 1 on the left to step 4 on the right of the chart in Figure 5.1.

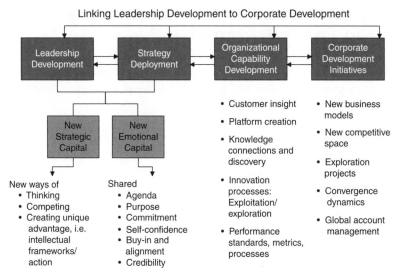

Linking Leadership Development to Corporate Development

FIGURE 5.1 Linking Leadership Development to Corporate Development

Option 2

We start with the logic of launching an exploration project, starting on the right-hand side of the chart in Figure 5.1. The sponsors of this exploration project will want to push the impact of this single project to the left, namely to see how insights can be scaled up into becoming new organizational capabilities and part of the strategic agenda. Finally, that new approach is becoming part of the leadership agenda.

Option 3

The middle-out approach: Here the initiative is coming from the strategy department to put ambidexterity on the agenda. Yes, they may initiate exploration projects directly, but they need ambassadors and a platform to bring ambidexterity into a wider context. Here is where an alliance between the organizational development and leadership development departments is important.

The Forum for Linking Leadership Development to Corporate Development

Academically the concept presented above may be quite solid and intellectually sound. However, it is the practicability that matters. Therefore, how and where do we get this started?

There are a number of possible approaches but let us focus on those four which usually turn up as candidates for providing the right forum for addressing the topic of ambidexterity:

- The strategic planning process.
- The budgeting process.
- The leadership development process.
- The CEO conference/top 75 conference.

Let us remember from Chapter 1 that for exploration projects we should be addressing innovation opportunities across the full spectrum of the ten types of innovation. That means ideally we should be expanding the bandwidth of the organization's innovation capability to encompass as many of these ten types as possible. It follows that we need to get as many stakeholders as possible engaged. So let us have a look at the viability for the options presented above.

we should be expanding the bandwidth of the organization's innovation capability

The strategic planning process

This would be the natural home for addressing the topic of ambidexterity. Usually, the top team and the strategic development experts, combined with some kind of bottom-up process from the individual businesses will come up with the strategic plan for the organization. The topic of ambidexterity should be embedded in this.

The challenge for ambidexterity: Usually great levels of comfort around exploitation and high levels of uncertainty around exploration. In particular, the requirement for exploration projects is not linked to internal individuals. Subsequently, if exploration is part of the strategic planning process, there is a quite high likelihood of outsourcing to external consultants.

The budgeting process

To put it bluntly: Most budget plans do not provide any allowance for exploration projects. Yes, in the first round, budgets for exploration projects may be there initially, but they are also the first candidates to be sacrificed in order to protect the core business, as the budget rounds get tighter and tighter. Therefore, budgets are disproportionally allocated to exploitation projects. Ultimately, any space for budget allocation to exploration projects is left to the very top of the organization. During the next financial year members of the top team may turn out to be the only ones who have the budget space to allocate support to exploration projects.

The leadership development process

In most organizations the leadership development processes are focusing on individual competence development, ensuring that individuals are prepared for their next level of career development. For the high potentials being prepared for general management roles a second objective is added: To create a cadre of executives from different functional areas who know each other and who can build on common trust to move the organization collectively into the future.

Oftentimes these high flyers programs are augmented with "action learning" projects. Sponsors are usually either the CEO or selected members of the top team. The objectives are generally twofold:

- To test the participants in a team working environment with high-level visibility.
- To push the strategic agenda to address in the project a topic that may not necessarily find a natural home in the usual organizational set-up.

My personal experiences are very mixed. I have seen superb contributions from teams who really felt that they were pushing the boundaries on behalf of the organization, supported by top management. On the other hand, I have also seen too many cases in which these projects were alibi exercises. The organization wanted to copy state-of-the-art learning organizations. Initially the intentions were good: However, when it came to picking topics for projects it became clear that these topics were taken from thin air, last minute, and were really not that relevant. The sponsors of these projects ended up doing a great disservice to both the individual participants and the learning and development (L&D) function.

The CEO conference/top 75 conference

The CEO conference is the usual annual gathering of the top 50–100 in large organizations. The usual format consists of key strategy announcements, some keynote speakers from the outside to instill controversy, exchange of best practice inside the organization, and some general team building activities. This is usually the one official forum, which brings together all the key people and the key functions.

So what is the right forum to address ambidexterity? Let us look at the options again in turn:

The strategic planning process: Intellectually great, but usually not related to individuals. Hence, exploration is often outsourced.

The budgeting process: Theoretically yes, but practically no. Individual budget holders are too incentivized to protect the current budget. Inadvertently also incentivized to support the current business, leading to exploitation projects.

The leadership development process: It brings together key talent from across functional areas with a view to building the next stage leadership cohort. It is focused on individual competence development and is often focused on general management. In theory, this is a great forum for launching exploration projects. However, drawbacks often consist in the lack of track record of L&D in strategy deployment and the often bad track record of projects allocated to participating teams.

Usually, the CEO/top 75 conference is focused on the CEO and on aligning the top team. The focus is on the general direction of the organization, rather than on specific projects.

So where does that leave us?

All the options discussed have their clear drawbacks. However, the top team around the CEO has still two additional options:

- To set up a special task force outside the normal organizational structures and processes.
- To outsource to external consultants.

In this book opportunities for building ambidextrous organizations are being investigated. Outsourcing to consultants is always an option. However, that option reduces the main organization to focusing on exploitation. Therefore, this chapter will focus on how to best connect the CEO conference, strategic planning, and L&D to enable exploration to take place within the organization.

Role of Corporate Universities – Teaching vs Research

So, let us look next at the most sophisticated form of L&D in an organization, the corporate universities (CUs).

For many years now, CUs have been in fashion. Jeanne C. Meister (1998) has been guiding much of the debate with academics and practitioners, mainly L&D experts. Now, when these CUs were initially set up, the previous portfolio of L&D was embedded in a larger context of a "university." The logic followed very much in the context of creating a "learning organization," as advocated in the early 1990s by Peter Senge (1990).

However, in most newly set up CUs the focus of the activities remained very strongly on "teaching" and "training." Of course the leaders of these

CUs debated in numerous conferences how to identify the relevant topics and how to be a meaningful "business partner" to the leaders in their organization. The EFMD, for example, has supported corporate programs over the years to increase both quality and relevance to the organizations through its CLIP program.

Traditional universities have a dual focus: Teaching and research. According to Wikipedia:

> A **university** (Latin: "universitas", "a whole") is an institution of higher education and research which grants academic degrees in a variety of subjects and provides both undergraduate education and postgraduate education. The word "university" is derived from the Latin universitas magistrorum et scholarium, which roughly means "community of teachers and scholars."

CUs have a strong tradition in teaching and training, but there is often little focus on "research." Here is the catch: With a focus on teaching, there is a clear link to "playing the existing game better." If the additional focus on research is not there, the room for "experimentation," "exploration," and "shaping game strategies" is heavily underutilized.

Corporate universities: Stages of sophistication

In the US CUs became famous through the well-publicized examples of GE's Crotonville and the Motorola University. The CUs at McDonald's and Disney also became famous for purposefully linking the strategic agenda of the organization to the mobilization of their people. The focus of these activities was on implementation of the corporate strategy.

In Europe, Thomas Sattelberger became one of the main drivers for CUs – first at Daimler Benz, then as founder of the Lufthansa School of Business, and later at Deutsche Telekom. He recently (2014) published a model indicating four stages in CU development:

1) Company specific management school focusing on individual competencies.
2) Engine for collective standardization.

3) Platform for and accelerator of corporate-wide top-down initiatives.
4) Cultural nucleus for organizational change processes.

However, Sattelberger concludes that a fifth stage should be required – prototype and lab for corporate renewal and innovation. In this model there is clearly a need for CUs to support experimentation with new strategies. This, in effect, adds the element of "research" to the already well-established track record of teaching to CUs.

In the language of this book the conclusion can be drawn that there is overwhelming evidence for successful contributions of CUs to exploitation, but also a lot of room for possible contributions to exploration. Therefore, we need to further investigate the purpose of a CU: To develop individual competencies and/or the organization's capabilities?

The Role of Competencies and Capabilities

In this book we look at ambidexterity from both an organizational perspective and an individual leadership perspective. When you try to look at these two perspectives through the development lens, you get two dimensions:

• Individual development with a focus on individual competencies.
• Organizational development with a focus on organizational capabilities.

When investigating the linkages between individual and corporate development and ideally finding a good balance between the two, we need to better understand these two dimensions.

According to Wikipedia:

> **Competence** is the ability of an individual to do a job properly. A competency is a set of defined behaviors that provide a structured guide enabling the identification, evaluation and development of the behaviors in individual employees.

Some scholars see "competence" as a combination of practical and theoretical knowledge, cognitive skills, behavior and values used to improve performance; or as the state or quality of being adequately or well qualified, having the ability to perform a specific role. For instance, life, management competency might include systems thinking and emotional intelligence, and skills in influence and negotiation.

Wikipedia defines capabilities as follows:

Enterprises consist of a portfolio or matrix of capabilities that are used in various combinations to achieve outcomes. Within that portfolio, a capability will be transient unless managed and maintained over time.

Whilst "competencies" are focused on the individual, "capabilities" are focused on the organization. Capabilities refer to the embedded processes in an organization such as new product development, recruitment, manufacturing, and so on. C. K. Prahalad (2000, personal conversation) nicely summarizes the distinction: "Capabilities stay on, when the competencies have gone home at night."

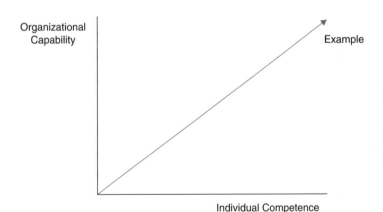

FIGURE 5.2 / Corporate Universities: Focus over Time

The organization according to the graph in Figure 5.2 would have to push in parallel the individual competencies and corporate capabilities dimensions. Now, this is a tall order. Let us look at the dimensions in detail.

Corporate Universities: Competencies and Capabilities

Competencies

Most organizations have over time developed quite sophisticated competence models. This is very much in line with the general advances in professionalism within the field of human resource (HR) management. Through competence models the organization tries to professionalize and standardize their expectation regarding employee selection and performance review of certain jobs, management, and leadership roles. Organizations such as The Hay Group, Lominger, and Kienbaum have built significant track records and expertise to support organizations in developing the specific competence model relevant for a given business or specific job category.

Through assessment processes, it is then relatively straightforward to conduct a gap analysis at the individual level and collectively at the organizational level. So, through the individual competence analysis, the development needs for an individual in his/her current role and/or for a future role can be identified. Through on or off the job development activities the gaps identified can be closed. With thorough HR support the individual can then identify the most suitable set of development activities. For example: In engineering driven organizations engineers have to learn about finance to be able to move into general management functions.

When you aggregate the individual analyses across a whole organization you can see the pattern of strengths and weaknesses. For example, in an engineering organization it would be expected to see a pattern of collective strengths in the competence of "logical thinking," but simultaneously a pattern of weaknesses in the competence of "financial acumen."

Now, let us take the competency perspective when building a CU. If the logic for the CU was very much driven by a competence perspective, the CU would focus on supporting the better understanding of financial acumen by setting up self-assessment and online finance learning tools. Also, the CU would link up with the best finance teachers to design, develop, and deliver first rate customized (to industry and organization) learning experiences.

Performance criteria for the CU are:

- *x* per cent of candidates attended.
- Competence before and after.
- Enjoyment of learning experience.
- Kirkpatrick's four stage model (reaction – learning – behavior – results).

Now, how would a CU driven by a competence perspective address the topic of ambidexterity?

Yes, there would be investment in an assessment tool, which may check for preferred leadership competencies relevant to both exploitation and exploration. In the existing assessment tools, we will most likely find a bias towards exploitation, mirroring the focus in current competence models. So the activities in designing the new assessment tool will be more focused on exploration.

In exploration you would probably see more emphasis on competencies such as:

- Dealing with ambiguity.
- Interpersonal savvy.
- Influencing others.

Then, how do you teach and develop ambidexterity? Surely not in the classroom! Action learning and real projects are required.

Capabilities

Capabilities are more than the aggregated individual competencies. The key is connecting individual competencies in a new way, creating robust, enforceable processes around them.

Capabilities are more than the aggregated individual competencies

Sometimes it is straightforward to identify new capabilities that are required. For instance, when the top management in your organization has declared that in the future the organization should move from ball bearing manufacturing to being an integrated component supplier, it is very obvious that the capability of "integrating" has to be high on the agenda. Likewise, when an insurance company changes its name from *xyz* Insurance to *xyz* Financial Services, promising its clients integrated financial services solutions, it is obvious that somehow the insurance experts and, for instance, the asset management experts will have to create new solutions, processes, and, in short, capabilities.

How can a CU then build new capabilities such as integration or solutions? In the competencies field discussed above, it is quite obvious to identify the topic of finance and to develop a robust development structure for it. In the capabilities field the challenge is at least twofold:

- There are few courses on integration or on solutions.
- Building capabilities requires more than individual development, it requires collective development.

Developing competencies can be driven very much by the individual. Developing capabilities, by definition, has to be a collective effort.

So, let us examine the implications for CUs in developing capabilities. At least three dimensions have to be considered:

- Who has to participate?
- What is the topic/framework of the concrete capability?
- How should the capability development be addressed?

The above list is not exhaustive, however. The "why" question is critical here. This is different from the competencies perspective. Let us revisit the example of the engineer scoring low in "finance acumen." If his/her aim is to move into a general management role in the future, will that individual ask why he/she has to close this gap? Of course not, as it is very plausible that understanding finance is integral to the role of a general manager. Many of the competency gaps can be rationally explained and it is quite likely that, maybe at first reluctantly, but then with verve, the engineer will close the competency gap.

In capability development, explicitly addressing the "why" question is critical. Why is it that our organization has to embrace new capabilities? In Chapter 1 we looked at the Kotter model for change processes. The first hurdle identified is the "sense of urgency" – therefore, an important task for the CU has to be to create a forum for the participants to understand "why" they can no longer stay in the safe environment of ball bearings or insurance.

Outside contributors may help to create a sense of urgency by pointing out some unavoidable facts and figures about changes in the environment. But there are limits to what extent the creation of a sense of urgency can be outsourced. The participants want to see their leaders on stage. They want to see their passion and convincing case for creating new capabilities. They are not expecting all the answers to be there already. They want to hear that their contribution is required. And yes, in building new capabilities there will be trial and error, as the organization collectively ventures into new, unfamiliar territory.

Sense of urgency

The CU has to possibly run a number of events in close succession to create the critical mass of individuals who share the sense of urgency. Video conferencing and mass gatherings can create an initial consistent message. The why questions however, cannot be fully dealt with in this format. A number of subsequent strategic dialogues are required during which the why questions, in smaller group settings, can be seriously addressed.

Leadership coalition

For the CEO and the top team it is critical to win the hearts and minds of the people in the next organizational layer. Therefore, the creation of settings that allow intimate, trustful discussions is essential. The CEO and the senior executives also have to be in listening mode, this is the time to elicit the resistance, questions, and uneasiness which are there anyway. This is where "fireside meetings" come in. This is the intimate setting in which the CEO or a member of the top team can sit down with an important few and talk honestly and directly, off the record.

The notion of fireside meetings is in many organizations overused, and is often extended to include top executive discussions in a classroom setting. This setting is too clinical. There is the need for a real fireside meeting, to lay the foundation for a strong leadership coalition based on trust.

Role of the fireside meeting

Many organizations that have focused on competency development already have a tradition of fireside meetings. However, in the competence setting the focus of the fireside meeting is on personal accord and on building a personal relationship across hierarchies with the high potentials.

The focus of fireside meetings in the setting of capability development is different. The focus is no longer on the individual but on building a strong leadership coalition. This means the executives addressing the participants as a group. Now, most organizations have a forum for these fireside chats. At one time in Daimler Benz it was the "Stuben" in Haus Lämmerbuckel; for another CEO it was important to have a setting in which to have a cigar. Each organization and the respective leaders have their own way of creating the level of intimacy required.

However, the fireside meetings do have a potential downside for both the participants and the leaders: For both parties there is the acute risk of being found out. Found out in terms of not being up to the task. I remember one occasion when, as members of the management boards took their turn, one participant in the fireside meeting said immediately afterwards: "Jens, can you please make sure that this guy does not get anywhere near an analyst…" It had been clearly exposed that this particular senior leader had not understood the new strategic direction. It was not long after this incident that this person left the organization. In fireside meetings people want to see authenticity, not boardroom speak.

From sense of urgency via leadership coalition into action

Chapter 8 will address the process architectures for successful ambidexterity in detail. Therefore, in this chapter it is only the intent to highlight the importance of the fact that a CU can create an infrastructure in which exploration can take place.

Once the CU has built the credibility for addressing the sense of urgency and has supported the out of office environment to foster a strong leadership coalition, the next challenge is to provide the platform for creating real projects. For instance, for the purpose of creating exploration projects at a CU a two- or three-day workshop should encompass the following:

Ideation: To purposefully create candidates for exploration projects; focusing on key projects and allocating potential project leaders.

Shaping: The development of the concrete idea into a project format, defining outcomes, milestones, roles and responsibilities, and initial resources required.

Decision: To obtain the go ahead from a senior executive in the role of project sponsor.

Now, the CU probably has access to good process facilitators, the organizational sponsor would have given guidance on topics to be addressed – functional experts such as market researchers and/or strategic planning would have provided the real background data. An outside input regarding the nature of ambidexterity and the difference in exploitation and exploration may be very helpful.

This is no longer teaching, this is workshop modus, this is facilitation, and this is co-creation. The setting is no longer an auditorium with fixed seats, all eyes looking to the front at the teacher or the CEO.

Symbols matter

Some organizations have chosen to build their corporate universities mirroring what their top executives experienced at leading business schools like Harvard or London. In the physical space of that CU you then find an auditorium in the style of an amphitheater. This comes with fixed chairs and all the focus on the stage, where presumably the lecturer will communicate his/her wisdom to the learners. This is a very good setting for building individual competence. However, it is not very helpful for building organizational capabilities. For that to happen, the "learners" should not focus on the lecturer but should be enabled and encouraged to interact with each other.

The many CUs I have visited usually had "seminar rooms" rather than "lab rooms." Symbols matter.

Exploration meetings in the boardroom

Working with one top team in a traditional business, the CEO – for reasons of time efficiency or other reasons – insisted on having the exploration meetings in the organization's boardroom. You can imagine: Big oak table, comfortable chairs, and pictures of previous chairpersons on the wall, with the CEO at the top of the table. The usual beamer was in place, so that everyone can see the presentation. It was a big surprise then, when there was no slide presentation, and instead some flip charts to capture the ideas. "But it is our style to have slide presentations, also in our exact corporate format." For exploration projects, the boardroom setting is inappropriate. Symbols matter.

Performance criteria for the CU

As the application of the CU is expanded to move beyond the focus on individual competencies to include organizational capabilities, the performance criteria have to be adjusted (Table 5.1)

Table 5.1 shows that the performance criteria have shifted very much from a consumption modus towards a call to action modus. It is no longer about: Did our executives enjoy the program/the experience? It is much

TABLE 5.1   Performance Criteria for Corporate Universities

Competencies	Capabilities
• X% of candidates attended	Sense of urgency?
• Competence before and after	Strong leadership coalition
• Enjoyment of learning experience	Are the participants up for it?
• 4-stage Kirkpatrick model	Ready to move into exploration projects in a structured format?

more about: Do we think that the participants are willing and able to take on the challenges?

From a capability perspective, the role of the CU shifts from a teaching and learning perspective to a "real" university experience. In real/normal universities the activities never just focus on teaching. Universities are about the thoughtful combination of original research and teaching. Now, what is the equivalent of original research in the context of CUs?

Research in real universities is about exploring new frontiers of knowledge; it is about testing hypotheses. It is about experimenting, failing, and succeeding. Everyone who has done a PhD knows about dealing with ambiguity. However, over the centuries real universities have found smart ways of reducing the risks for both a PhD student and the university. The PhD supervisor acts as the sponsor, the PhD community, guided usually by a set of compulsory research courses, provide the scaffolding for reducing the risk.

This is the analogy for what a CU should do in its role as university – balance teaching and research. The heavy focus on teaching should be strengthened by establishing solid scaffolding for research, namely exploration.

Development of CUs over time – case examples

Over the last 30 years when working with early examples of CUs – sometimes as an architect, sometimes as a contributor, facilitator, consultant, teacher, or program director – I have had the chance to observe the long-term impact. Just to launch a CU does not create success, what happens after the first successful sessions? Ambidexterity?

I would like to provide a few case examples to illustrate generic patterns I have observed, which may be helpful for the reader to ascertain how to best use or further develop a CU in the context of ambidexterity.

To illustrate the cases and to provide a framework in which to discuss each one, Figure 5.3 demonstrates the two dimensions:

- Individual competence.
- Organizational capability.

In these case examples I want to illustrate how different patterns emerged over a period of time:

Packaging/manufacturing: This is an example of almost a straight 45 degree line to simultaneously address individual competence and organizational capabilities.

Bank: As an example of a corporate leadership institute which over a four-year period, consequently in 30 global workshops, focused

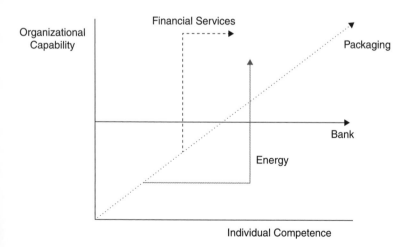

FIGURE 5.3 **Case Examples: Corporate Universities**

on individual global leadership competencies. However, the focus remained on the competencies dimension.

Financial services: As an example of starting with capability, then after economic crisis moving back to competence.

Energy management: As an example of focusing on competencies, then shooting into the capability realm to settle on the 45 degree line.

These examples have been chosen to reflect actual patterns rather than to suggest that one approach is better than another; in order to illustrate the potential bandwidth for CUs.

BOX 5.1 CASE EXAMPLE: PACKAGING/MANUFACTURING

This case contains original extracts from the case submitted to the European case writing competition EFMD Excellence in Practice Award 2014 by Amcor Flexibles Europe and America (AFEA) & University St Gallen Executive School of Management.

How AMCOR Flexibles Europe and Americas (AFEA) and ES-HSG are Driving Organisational Professionalism

Executive Summary

In 2012, Amcor Flexibles Europe and Americas (AFEA) – Amcor's biggest Business Group and one of the world's leading Flexible packaging manufacturers – kicked off its successful leadership development program with the University of St. Gallen's Executive School of Management, Technology and Law.

Shortly before the launch, the AFEA team realized that in order to ensure successful future development they needed to further advance with the leadership capabilities of the organization. This suggested that they needed to revitalize their focus on developing their talent and build stronger individual competencies alongside their competitive capabilities to take the business to the next level, create a culture of outperformance and accelerate profitable growth.

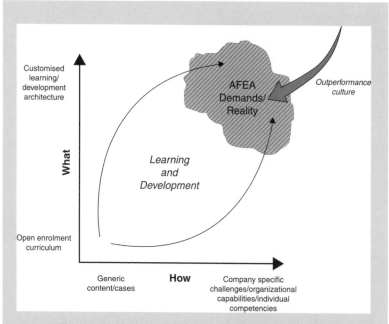

FIG 5.4 Amcor AFEA's Demand Plotted within the Environment of Executive Education and Leadership Development Measures

With Human Resources and Senior Management at AFEA completely involved and the Business Group President committed to make this initiative not only a support for further Leadership development of the organization's managers with potential, but to also strengthen the organization's outperformance culture, the program enabled AFEA to continue to build their leadership capabilities.

Designed as a three modular leadership program, "Lead to Outperform II" (LTO II) looked into the aspects of Leading Self, Leading Teams and Leading the Business. It was meant to embrace the Amcor Leadership Competency Framework and accelerate the processes of its implementation. With residential modules, inter-modular activities, the setup of an Individual Development Plan (integrating measurable links to business performance) and the creation of the right Human Resources

Support Infrastructure, the learning architecture was not only tailored to AFEA's demands but could witness a day-to-day practicality in the participants' environment.

The LTO II Program in partnership with St. Gallen therefore acted as a catalyst for:

- Implementing the expected leadership behaviors/competencies at the individual level
- Developing new organizational capabilities (IDP, 360°, HR-community, etc.)
- Providing meaning to the "outperformance" culture and to demonstrate measureable business impact.

Results and impact could be measured on the individual as well as on the organizational level, the latter more precisely confirming improvements regarding financials and applied processes. Be it the installment of a 360°-feedback procedure or considerable reduction of waste in some areas, be it the regaining of focus in leadership and the improvement of decision making or the beneficial interaction of colleagues between Europe and the United States – outperformance culture was fostered.

Overall, the experience of the Amcor/St. Gallen partnership showed and shows the alignment of demanding strategic objectives with professional, robust development processes as a potential step for making a difference.

Final Reflection

After a period of consolidation, AFEA recognized the requirement to strengthen its leadership capabilities as one of the foundations to the "outperformance" culture. The Amcor Leadership Competency Framework provided the conceptual underpinning for the expected leadership behaviors and leadership development processes, and Human Resources were prepared to make a difference.

The successful implementation of a leadership development program which strengthened the focus on talent in the organization and which could be monitored in clear results showed that the approach chosen was the right one. It has been recognized as a program, which added value to not only the participants individually, but also to the business. There are clear examples of an immediate impact on the business results, processes and alignment and even beyond that, 10 out of the 35 participants of the first cohort have been promoted to a different role.

It has been a rewarding start of building and establishing an AFEA development portfolio, to address development needs of AFEA's co-workers as part of its talent management and performance management approach. The development portfolio is currently being expanded with specific functional training programs and online learning solutions to address key capabilities, which are required for the organization to continue to grow and be successful.

Summing up, the success of the impactful LTO II-program can be related to three particularities within the organization:

1) **Using strategic agenda.** The notion of the strategic "outperformance"-targets was equally transferred to Leadership Development including measurable impact on the business.

2) **Developing corporate capabilities & individual competencies.** Both "Leadership Development" and "Capability Development" were equally introduced in this program. The program started with "Leading Self", purposefully allowing new corporate capabilities be developed and implemented around: Individual Development Plans (IDP), 360°-feedback process, HR-support groups, e-learning tools, and Web-based conferencing. LTO II was designed to allow the development and enhancement of these corporate capabilities. Moreover, individual competencies have been strengthened and developed – all in the light of the Amcor Leadership

Competency Framework. The number of participants already promoted supports the program's constructive outcome.

3) **Senior management demand & support.** Consistent application of "outperformance"-culture could and can be observed. In that respect the Business Group President has been clear in his demand that at the very beginning each IDP should be explicitly linked to performance goals. The case demonstrates that outperformance goals were met, at both organizational and individual levels. Regarding the support of the program, senior management presence has been visible in all modules and resulted in strong buy-in and motivation of all participants.

"The Lead to Outperform II program has contributed considerably to creating a development culture and approach within AFEA. It has shown an immediate and positive impact on the business as well as the individual careers of the participants.

Finally it has contributed to creating a network of senior managers across our organization which will continue to strengthen our Outperformance Culture and making each other successful across business units and functions."

AFEA Vice President Human
Resources & Communications

Through the launch of the Leadership Development programs AFEA has been able to build a more integrated development portfolio of learning solutions. And adding to leadership development, the organization has established – and is still building – specific functional development portfolios, focusing on technical and functional skills, e-learning programs and other virtual learning solutions, etc. which are all supporting the development needs of AFEA's co-workers and linking them to their performance objectives and outcomes of talent management reviews. Finally, the Development Portfolio responded/responds to a need, which was raised through the global "Engagement Survey" in 2012, stating that there was not sufficient focus on people development in the organization.

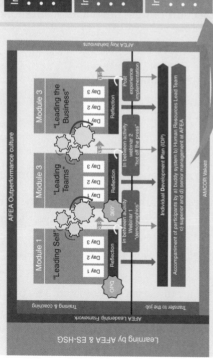

"Outperformance" in impact...

Impact on "corporate level" (performance)
- Financial results
- Waste reduction improvements
- Increased competitiveness

Impact on "individual level" (competency)
- Better understanding one's effect on others
- Change in position according to strength profiles
- Promotion of managers due to programme outcome

Impact on "processes level" (capability)
- Introduction of the *Individual Development Plan*
- Introduction of the *360°-Feedback process*
- Introduction of the *Buddy System*

... and in an **increase in the relevance of HR!**

Fig 5.5 The Three-Level Impact of the LTO II-Program

The presence of the Business Group President and other members of the Executive Management Team during the program added to the success of the initiative. The fact that AFEA had other Vice Presidents to present to the group during the face-to-face modules has shown the level of executive buy-in, which according to the Vice President Human Resources & Communications has been key to the success of the program.

BOX 5.2 CASE EXAMPLE: BANK

In this global financial services organization the task was very clear. Right after the Lehmann crisis a global financial services provider launched their global leader program. It was global in the sense that the locations covered financial centers in Europe, New York, Singapore, and Hong-Kong. The structure of the program is a reflection of the Marshall Goldsmith global leader concept.

The topics identified are:

- Building partnerships and alliances.
- Sharing leadership.
- Cultural diversity.
- Thinking globally.
- Strategic technological savvy.
- Innovation – as an all-encompassing undercurrent.

There were forty participants for two days in their home location, with three faculty members covering these topics. In total, 30 programs were delivered. In each program a discussion on current strategic issues was conducted with a senior local business leader.

More than 800 senior directors participated. The outcome was a significant increase in the level of awareness of the topics. The results generated the insight that the innovation landscapes for businesses such as investment banking, asset management, and private banking looked very similar independent of location! There was usually a big surprise when we showed the analyses of previous groups in different locations. For example, in the case of a small special business unit represented in all locations it was very insightful to realize that independently from each other the leaders in each location shared the same perceptions in terms of innovation patterns and innovation opportunities.

Technological savvy: The prevailing view of the senior directors regarding the role of IT was that it provides the plumbing rather than the strategic direction akin to the role of an architect. What hampered the transition: Reputation of IT function and personal standing of IT experts as plumbers. On the side of the other Directors, the lack of understanding of IT's potential, lack of technical know-how.

The organization was content with the fact that 800 managing directors improved their individual competencies. No attempt was made to extend the mandate to connect the individual competencies to create new organizational capabilities.

The results were:

- Consistently high participant feedback.
- Renewal of contract with client over a period of four years.

BOX 5.3 CASE EXAMPLE: SERVICES

The Company is operating in the energy management sector. The organization is owned by private equity investors and has recently installed a new management team.

The ambidexterity challenge they face is to exploit their existing customer base based on established long-term contracts. At the same time, the organization wants to explore opportunities in global energy markets. New business models must be tested deliberately in non-core markets.

The Company has 4,000 employees, operating in over 20 countries. The general management program, targeted at the top 40 in the organization and the next 40, was made up of the following components:

- Strategy; value creation.
- Finance.
- Leadership.
- Innovation/change.

The difference in the approach between top 40 and next 40 was based primarily around the strategic focus vs the implementation focus. As a result of the general management program, all top 80 were aligned around concepts, language, and experiences. Role of top 40: spearheading the move from national champion to global organization.

Upon completion of the various modules of the general management program, the organization formally launched the CU. The activities at the university were directly linked to the strategic agenda of the organization.

In the first two years after inauguration five company-specific case studies were written. The cases were no more than five pages long and covered either best practice or a turnaround situation. These strategic cases were in each case supported by an elaborated financial spreadsheet model, allowing the participants to conduct a sophisticated "what if" analysis of the options considered. University researchers or faculty did not write the five cases, they were authored by members of the top management team. This allowed senior executives to explicitly describe the leadership challenges they saw and provide the basis for concrete and implementable solutions.

The cases were used both at the top management conference and at university meetings to develop solutions that were then subsequently owned by the top 80 management team. This overall approach is certainly a vivid example of successfully linking individual leadership development and corporate development. However, it also provided a solid platform for demonstrating ambidexterity: Exploiting best practice and scaling it out to global markets, using exploration in remote countries to create proof of concept.

BOX 5.4 CASE EXAMPLE:
FINANCIAL SERVICES

The Zurich Development Center was opened in 1999. It is a physical manifestation of the alignment of the strategic agenda with a move from insurance to financial services and the CU approach.

At the time, the organization had a strong tradition of leadership development and alignment between strategic agenda and leadership development. Witness the Roadmap, the well-documented strategic planning tool. The Roadmap mirrored state of the art of strategic thinking and modeling, reflecting key business school concepts and the latest strategic consultancy thinking. It provided the application of these concepts to the insurance industry and to Zurich Insurance in particular.

The Roadmap served as the backbone for strategic decision making and the annual strategic planning process. In order to get the Roadmap embedded in the organization, a standardized training concept was implemented through a group of internal consultants. In parallel, at the executive level, leadership development was implemented in association with a host of business schools ranging from Kellogg to Boccioni. The topics addressed in these customized leadership programs mirrored the Roadmap, covering strategic analysis, market segmentation, and finance.

When I joined as head of capability development in January 1998, already 1,000 of the Zurich executives had completed the executive program and the CEO challenged me with three immediate tasks:

1) Development of a new HR strategy.

2) Identification of a site for the Zurich Development Center, the CU.

3) Development of a new leadership program.

What had prompted the CEO, and the top team, to fundamentally review key aspects of their already highly effective development infrastructure? The answer was very clear: The name of the organization was changed in August 1998 from Zurich Insurance to Zurich Financial Services. This was not just a cosmetic brand development exercise; it was a reflection of a significant strategic decision to move from insurance to developing customer solutions in financial services. This was also well supported with mergers and acquisitions to include asset management.

At the turn of the century we saw huge strategic challenges in particular around the Internet application and the emergence of new market players such as AOL. These new contenders received a significant higher stock market evaluation compared to organizations in traditional businesses such as insurance. One hallmark was to look at the number of customer relationships. At the height of the Internet bubble the market capitalization of AOL per client was factor x.

So how does the organization now compete in financial services instead of insurance? At the time a whole host of new concepts for financial services were tested, bringing together banking and insurance companies, (e.g. CS and Winterthur Insurance), the music and airline industries (e.g. Virgin), and supermarkets (e.g. Tesco and Marks and Spencer in the UK).

One thing was very clear to me right at the beginning of 1998: Playing the existing game better was not an option. As we conducted the needs and gaps analysis, inside and outside the organization (with the management team, HR, customers, headhunters, competitors, and analysts), it became very clear that we had to engage in shaping game strategies.

After four LEAD 1 workshops the feedback from the participating executives was overwhelming. It was not so much that they liked the workshops, indeed we never applied a formal happy sheet, but the participants stressed the relevance of the discussions had. This was witnessed by the fact that outside of the sessions par- ticipants mailed the materials to their teams. Word got around and after four months, four workshops, and some 100 participants, the feedback was very clear: We cannot just talk about it, we have to do it for real!

We cannot just talk about it, we have to do it for real!

This is when we launched the second module: Innovation. In total 71 innovation concepts were launched, nine were implemented.

External visibility

In Zürich and London, fifteen innovation concepts were pre- sented. Four of the concepts came through the LEAD process. The feedback from investors and analysts was that they get it – they are ahead of the pack! The share price during these two days went up 10 per cent. At the time that was an equivalent of $4 billion: Quite an impressive level of trust offered towards the organization.

Strategic significance

The initial innovation concepts highlighted the need for cross business unit collaboration. Subsequently, we saw the launch of practice boards to shift the country-based CEO structure: Initially for functional areas such as IT and HR and customer groups such as retail, commercial, and corporate customers. The task of these practice boards was to identify areas for cross BU cooperation. We used the LEAD faculty to work with the practice boards to define their strategic agenda.

Whilst the initial LEAD program was focusing on individual development, with LEAD II and the work with the practice boards the logic had long since moved from individual development to organizational development.

Semantics matter!

In the case of the Zurich Development Center, there was a conscious choice not to call it the CU. At the management board meeting, when the funding for the Center had to be decided, I could not make a business case for training and development alone. That could have been done much more cost effectively in hotels or at business schools. Then the key question was asked: "Where does research and development in financial services take place?"

Conclusions

In this chapter the opportunity to purposefully link individual and corporate development was investigated. The strategic planning and budgeting processes are natural candidates to support the building of an ambidextrous organization. However, the track record seems to indicate that both processes by themselves are not adequate to support ambidexterity. The chapter then subsequently focused on the leadership development process as a source for building ambidextrous organizations.

A large part of this chapter looked at the role of a CU. This is of course an extreme form of leadership development, which is most likely to be applied by large organizations. Although, over the years we have also witnessed many smaller organizations moving this way.

Why focus on CUs instead of just leadership development? The term "university" is critical to our debate on "ambidexterity." Ambidexterity refers to both exploitation and exploration: Universities are equally engaged in two core activities – teaching and research. In terms of a "corporate" university the link is immediately obvious:

- Exploitation – teaching.
- Exploration – research.

Therefore, by definition a "corporate university" can provide the glue between the individual development process and the corporate development process.

Now, in your organization you may not have a CU and there might not even be a plan to build one. However, if you take it as a concept that symbolically can combine the two processes of leadership development and corporate development you should see the opportunities for linking them.

This chapter has investigated the role of CUs in establishing ambidexterity in organizations. The observation is that currently the focus rests very much on supporting exploitation, running the existing game better. This is largely driven by the fact that CUs are usually run from an HR perspective. In HR a lot of progress has been made to professionalize the processes of talent identification and development. For years the mantra was that HR becomes a strategic partner to implement business strategies – and HR succeeded.

Therefore, competency models were developed to reflect the strategic requirements of the organization. The competency models were then translated into assessment tools to identify and select top talent. Development activities through the CU then functioned as a means to close the individual's competence gap in say, financial acumen.

However, in terms of ambidexterity CUs may become the victims of their own success. In terms of developing the curriculum for the university to reflect the strategy, many became deeply embedded in the "teaching" role of a university, supporting the exploitation hand. CUs have to find their role to support exploration in an organization. Sattelberger (2014) has pointed out the opportunity CUs provide to include labs and business model testing. However, before creating any lab activities around specific projects there is a need to create a sense of urgency and a strong leadership alliance.

What are the implications of this for a CU?

- They have to stay relevant in providing the forum for strategic debate, a strategic dialogue in an organization.
- CUs have to provide the platform to debate the why question inside the organization. If that debate is held outside the CU, it means it has lost its strategic relevance.
- They have to become the trusted partner linking top management and the next leadership layers.
- CUs have access to world-class faculty who can support the strategic dialogue, demonstrating that top team agenda is aligned with global developments.
- They have to foster an honest strategic dialogue. Now, dialogue is different from teaching. Without a proper dialogue, the why question will not be addressed and will simmer under the surface.

HR, for more than 20 years, also followed the mantra of Senge, to create the learning organization. This is very much in line with being the strategic partner to the business, to support the implementation of business strategies.

In terms of ambidexterity, with a focus on supporting exploration projects, HR and CUs have to play an active role to challenge orthodoxies. As C. K. Prahalad (2010) challenged us, we should not think so much about the learning organization, but focus on the forgetting organization.

How can CUs therefore transition from a strategic partner to becoming the source of new strategic thinking? In this the CUs would really adopt the "university" perspective, namely to challenge current thinking and explore new frontiers of corporate knowledge.

6

Solution: Scouting – Looking Beyond

Why is this Important for You and for Your Organization?

In your role as architect or project manager you need to understand the opportunities of scouting as drivers for exploration processes and idea generation in principle. You are very familiar with the normal data regarding market research, trends in the industry, and market shares. On that basis you are also fully acquainted with forecasting or predicting market developments, which you can then use as input for your internal planning activities.

In exploration processes you are literally in unchartered territory. Instead of playing an existing game better you are in shaping game territory and instead of predicting or forecasting, your talent in creating a point of view is required. How can you create a point of view, on what basis? Clearly, you have to do some reconnaissance to look beyond. Now, reconnaissance is very much associated with the military and therefore it is unsurprising that I have not yet in a business context met a person who has been introduced to me as the "chief reconnaissance officer." However, it is much more likely to find people with titles such as "head of technology scouting." This chapter will talk about technology scouting as one form of scouting. However, there are a number very practical tools that can help you to create that point of view.

At the organizational level, the processes and the organizational commitment should be present to make scouting possible. Importantly, it should not have to rely on the random achievement of an individual project leader, but must be purposefully installed as a corporate capability.

Fast Second: Scouting as Implementing a Strategic Choice

In their book *Fast Second* Markides and Geroski (2004) make an important point for large organizations. They conclude that, because big companies lack capability in exploration processes, they should rely on start-ups to do the exploration. Once a dominant design is emerging, then the large organization should step in and use their exploitation capabilities to scale up the new businesses.

So what can an organization actually do, if they make this strategic decision: To leave exploration to be done outside the organization? Clearly they have to build scouting capabilities. This implies that they have inside experts monitoring and scouting for emerging patterns.

What are these patterns? In this section we will focus, as an example, on patterns in technology. For technology patterns, the Gartner Hype Cycle (Wheatley, 2014) has become quite a useful gauge to identify at what stage of applicability a given technology is. The hype cycle depicts how the expectations regarding a new technology develop over time. The cycle distinguishes the following phases:

• Innovation trigger.
• Peak of inflated expectations.

- Trough of disillusionment.
- Slope of enlightenment.
- Plateau of productivity.

As this hype cycle is updated regularly, the individuals in charge of technology scouting have a good knowledge of the expectations related to individual new technologies.

Now, the hype cycle provides access to an evaluation of a given technology. But if scouting is to be successful, individual players in this technology have to be identified. Does the organization know who the drivers are; does it have access to them? Scouting, as a way of implementing the fast second strategy, will only work when these two questions can be answered positively.

For individuals in charge of technology scouting the implications are that they have to build a robust network of reliable sources often on a global scale. It also means attending the important global conferences and fairs on the technologies scouted.

Examples of technology scouting

Many organizations support their scouting activities by purposefully inviting start-up companies to approach them. Companies, such as Novartis in the pharmaceutical industry, are proactively offering collaborative partnerships. This is similar to the concept of crowd sourcing, as introduced in Chapter 3 with the examples of Dell and Starbucks. However, this form of scouting is different in that it is not the idea itself that is the focus. The aim is to elicit the personal introduction of the start-up company and their players. This then becomes the basis for purposefully discussing avenues of collaboration.

The insurance company Axa in Germany is taking this one step further. They have set up the Axa innovation campus, which allows the start-up companies to go through a rigorous process of initial development of the business concept and provides the opportunity for funding in a structured way.

In those organizations with a technology scouting department, I have observed a very mixed picture in recent years. On the positive side, yes there are some straight home runs when the scouting department is able to successfully broker collaboration between a start-up and the organization. Usually only the collaboration as such is being publicly reported on. The exact details of how the collaboration came about is not much talked about, could be an injustice to the technology scouting experts who may have done all the hard work in the background.

On the negative side, the stories are much more vivid, perhaps unfair to the members of technology scouting units. Start-ups are easily attracted by the big brand name of the scouting organization. They will eagerly polish their business case and their presentations. They may even sign legal documents to provide exclusivity to the scouting organization. However, I have observed that many times the culture clash between the two organizations' mindsets becomes apparent: The nimble, fast moving start-up on one side and, on the other, the slow moving large organization with processes, lawyers, lawyers, and lawyers…

Once the start-up has started negotiations with the scouting organization, it is very much at the mercy of the individuals in the technology scouting function. The start-up may have signed some legally binding documents with the technology scouting group, but they have no idea what happens after that. Yes, the department of technology scouting thinks it is a good idea, but how good are they in subsequently selling this idea to the decision makers inside the organization? Can they find a suitable sponsor? Can they find the budget? All of this is invisible to the start-up; it is now at the mercy of the organizational black box. It is not too difficult to imagine the potential for frustration.

Technology scouting in itself is a good platform from which to look beyond. However, its success depends so much on the people who are running that function, the department of "technology scouting." Do the key personnel have the ear of top management? Can they influence key decision makers across the organization? Can they keep the legal department in check so as not to scare away the start-up?

Many organizations, when installing a technology scouting department, purposefully bring in people from outside the company, if not even the industry, to broaden the company's horizons. However, the success of these individuals is not only dependent on identifying the right scouting targets, it is also dependent on their ability to work the internal politics of the organization.

I have observed too many examples of frustration between start-ups and large organizations, with the technology scouting department right in the middle. What does that lead to? The start-ups are frustrated by the lost time. Not immediately, but eventually when the negative stories make the rounds, it will also lead to the erosion of the scouting organization's credibility in the "community" of start-up companies. This eventually hampers the larger organization's ability to attract the necessary start-up contacts.

Frustration does then not only prevail at the start-up companies, but also among the people in the technology scouting department. They, often hired with high expectations on both sides, realize that the organization is not as ready as expected to embrace exploration. Now, they can still – for a while – enjoy attending global conferences, being exposed to the latest trends, creating valuable networks, and being the honored guests at all sorts of discussion panels, representing their organization.

How does the organization that made the strategic choice to be fast second feature in this? It may have a function called technology scouting, but has it been given enough airtime, visibility, and credibility? If the answer is no, it is not only the people responsible for technology scouting that have a problem, but the whole organization! If in effect the one bet on exploration is not working, the organization is quickly reduced to exploitation as their main source for innovation.

What is the solution? Technology scouting functions or departments are a good platform for engagement with start-ups. In order for that to work, the technology scouting functions should be given the appropriate level of sponsorship inside the organization. They should also have enough "political clout" on their side to ensure the rest of the organization listens to and respects them.

Difference between the Types of Businesses

As has been highlighted throughout this book so far, the general concept of ambidexterity consists of simultaneously engaging in exploitation and exploration. In exploitation you play the existing game better. You have chosen to play soccer and you have to train harder to serve the existing customers and to beat the known competition.

In exploration we are in shaping game territory. That means that we are not sure what the new game is or who our (new) competitors are.

Now, there must at least be some degree of certainty: Our customers! Surely, ambidexterity must be primarily about serving customers better, maybe in a different way. Now, what happens if through ambidexterity the definition of "customer" is also challenged?

For organizations serving customers directly, often called B2C (business to consumer), this challenge is not an issue. But for organizations operating in a B2B2C (business to business to consumer) format, the challenge is immense. For instance, as a manufacturer of electronic chips, of packaging material, or of building material, you usually have no direct contact with the end-users, such as the customers for a tablet computer, customers for pet food, or home owners for that matter.

In the 1990s, as some readers may well remember, Intel the chip-manufacturer ran global advertising campaigns with the catch phrase "Intel inside." Now, Intel was not selling the electronic chips to us as end-users, but in fact to Dell, HP, and IBM. These companies would then sell their PCs to us, the end-users. In marketing terms this can be called a "pull strategy," in that the end-users go to the retail outlet to ask for a PC with "Intel inside" and the retailers report back to the PC manufacturers that now Intel chips are in demand.

As Intel was spending all this money on advertising to the end-users, I am sure a lot of work was conducted to understand how effective this advertising spend was. What would Intel have to do to understand that effectiveness? Research with the end-users, talk to them about the advertising. Intel did exactly what other high spending consumer goods manufacturers, such as a PepsiCo or Coca-Cola, would do when checking the effectiveness of their advertising campaigns.

For me, Intel is a good example of how a B2B2C organization can engage in scouting. This means to move beyond their immediate business realm and in fact leap-frog one step in the value chain. Intel started this way back in the 1990s. However, they have kept that original momentum to this day, as we will see in examples a little bit later in this chapter.

Executives from organizations in a B2B2C environment realize that there are great opportunities beyond the immediate B2B step. However, to address that opportunity and to directly engage with the end-user is initially quite compelling. After an initial level of excitement though, it is very challenging to implement. You may recall the mindset challenges discussed in Chapter 4: "This is cannibalization, how can we make numbers next quarter when we are now by-passing our customers?" This is the normal immediate response. However, just look at the words being used, "by-passing our customers…" You can see immediately that now is the time to talk about who our "customers" are. Are they the distributors, manufacturers, retailers, or the end-users?

In many B2B2C settings in the last few years, new opportunities have arisen. These have been especially driven by new technology platforms, which allow the presentation of an organization's products and services to everyone including the end-users. This is in fact what Nespresso did more than 20 years ago to bypass retail and to build a direct customer relationship with the end-user. It may be the "Zeitgeist" or the work on innovation landscapes that leads executives in B2B2C organizations to realize that all their innovation focus goes into products and processes, which are geared towards their customer next in line. However, with an "Intel inside" approach they could focus on the end-user as customer, with implications for new customer experiences, new revenue models, new processes, and so on.

We are now all of a sudden struggling with the notion of who our "customers" are! Let's look at one recent example from a traditional industry that had built their success on having developed very strong links with distributors who would in turn deliver goods and services to the end-user in all the relevant global markets. They invariably view these distributors as their customers. Now, some big end-users approach this organization and ask in a forthright manner to build a direct relationship. With all the electronic platforms available, they ask, "Why can we not order directly from you?"

What may seem to be a simple request actually has huge ramifications inside the organization:

- Do we have the IT capabilities to serve customers directly?
- The sales people will ask: How can we make targets next quarter, if we now compete with our customers, that is, the distributors?
- The finance people will ask: How can we keep our differential pricing between markets, if prices are now transparent?
- The marketing people will be challenged to describe the buying behavior of these end-users.

In that particular workshop, all five new project proposals for exploration projects had one thing in common: To challenge the current distributor model.

Exploitation projects would not address that fundamental question. Exploration projects do. Therefore, the implication is that, in traditional B2B organizations, exploration projects inevitably address the issue of the relationship with the end-user. It is the Nespresso example that inspires individuals to challenge: Why can we not be the Nespresso in our industry?

Scouting: Open Innovation

As this chapter is about scouting – looking beyond – the opportunities around open innovation or crowd sourcing should be revisited. This means to purposefully investigate ideas coming from outside the organization and to augment them to our internal ideas. Chapter 3 has already looked at the opportunities for open innovation to significantly increase the number of ideas available to the organization. As discussed, Starbucks and Dell receive thousands of ideas from their customers, which they showcase on their Internet platforms Mystarbucks.com and www.ideastorm.com, respectively.

When teaching innovation I sometimes let participants purposefully investigate open innovation sites such as the ones from Dell and Starbucks. The reaction from my teaching audiences is very different: In open classes where we have participants from many organizations the response is usually: "Very good idea! We should also do that in my organization at home."

The reaction in the setting of an in-house innovation session, with participants from a single organization, is generally quite different. After the groups of participants understand the examples, the reaction usually is "Wow, this is impressive!" When I ask them to consider doing something similar in their own organization, the collective brainstorming sets in:

"It cannot possibly work in our industry. It is crazy; we cannot make these ideas public."

"All our competitors can see these as well! How can we handle so many ideas internally?"

"As our customers supply these ideas, how can we keep our promise to report on progress?

"Then, as we report progress, again our competitors can see our movements…"

In the end their conclusion is often that, yes, it is very interesting, but it cannot possibly work for us.

Now this reaction is a pity. Open innovation approaches achieve two things:

1) Engage loyal customers and make them feel valued over and beyond the products and services. This in fact creates a new level of customer experience for them and provides a solid backbone for a vibrant customer relationship.
2) Provide a huge number of ideas, augmenting the ideas already created inside the organization. Now, the number of ideas is not so much important in terms of the individual idea. It is important to be able to detect patterns. Large numbers allow you to see patterns in the ideas submitted; they reflect the "Zeitgeist" and allow you to respond on the basis of patterns rather than individual ideas.

The "Zeitgeist" very much prevails, as around the globe we all get the same information at the same time. Wikipedia and Google are providing free access to information on key topics, making it quite normal for ideas to be simultaneous – globally.

BOX 6.1 CASE EXAMPLE: SIMULTANEITY OF IDEAS

For one client we added an extra step to the three-day innovation workshop. At the end of the first day, when the 25 participants had already generated some 80 ideas, which later on were condensed to eight projects, we sent them off to enjoy dinner and a well-deserved glass of wine. You can imagine the excitement at the dinner table:

> "Eight ideas developed in one day that are absolutely unique! Can we start a little bit earlier tomorrow morning to get to work on these ideas in detail?"

Now, what the participants did not know was that the organizers had quickly summarized the eight ideas and sent them to a location some seven hours behind our time zone. During our night, there a group of researchers was ready to investigate the competitive landscape around these ideas.

The next morning all the participants were ready to work in their groups on the ideas they had prepared the previous day. After a short welcome, we handed out a "present" to each group: A short seven to ten page analysis of the competitive space for each project, produced during our night. After a few minutes of reading the documents there was stunned silence! All the euphoria of the night before had been blown away! What had happened? The project ideas, seen as being so unique the previous evening, turned out to be in fact quite common. This idea was implemented already in South Africa; some key competitor was testing something similar already in Finland; and so it went on. This is the effect of simultaneity of ideas.

With this particular client we could see this effect immediately and had a chance during the three-day workshop to come up with remedial action. Some projects had to be killed there and then, because no differential advantage could be seen. Other projects were re-shaped in a way that made the idea really unique.

Simultaneity of ideas is usually not seen in internal innovation workshops, as we use the frame of our own organization as the reference point for what is called "innovation." However, in innovation efforts we need to strive for uniqueness. As we do that, it does no harm to assume that someone around the globe is working on exactly the same idea as we are.

So how can we deal with the challenges of simultaneity of ideas? Open innovation! As displayed in the Starbucks and Dell examples, open innovation shows live to you and your organizations which ideas are popping up and what kind of patterns are emerging.

Scouting: Big Data as a Source for Looking Beyond

In organizations it is the most normal thing to use data for decision making. This is in fact what business schools have trained managers to do for many years. As this chapter is investigating sources for scouting, looking beyond we cannot miss the potential opportunities around "big data."

What is the difference between big data and what we are used to doing with data anyway, by way of normal business practice?

Big data is surely one of the buzzwords of our times. However, it may also hold a key to scouting, and to looking beyond. Let us investigate. Arguably, a hallmark of a buzzword is that everyone assumes to understand what is meant by it, only to find out that the opposite is the case. This was witnessed by a study conducted at Berkeley, which showed that, among some 43 top experts, there were a number of differing opinions on the definition of big data (Dutcher, 2014):

- Big data describes datasets that are so large, complex, or rapidly changing that they push the very limits of our analytical capability.
- Big data represents a cultural shift in which more and more decisions are made by algorithms with transparent logic, operating on documented immutable evidence.
- What's "big" in big data isn't necessarily the size of the databases, it's the big number of data sources we have, as digital sensors and behavior trackers migrate across the world. As we triangulate information in more ways, we will discover hitherto unknown patterns in nature and society – and pattern making is the wellspring of new art, science, and commerce.

Ok, that is a bit of a spread, so let us look for help in circles with final authority. Here is how the *Oxford English Dictionary* defines big data:

> data of a very large size, typically to the extent that its manipulation and management present significant logistical challenges.

Wikipedia defines big data as:

> an all-encompassing term for any collection of data sets so large and complex that it becomes difficult to process using on-hand data management tools or traditional data processing applications.

As you can see from these various vantage points, there is a lot of energy behind this topic. I would like to add two additional perspectives on big data provided by Gil Press (2014):

The belief that the more data you have the more insights and answers will rise automatically from the pool of ones and zeros.

A new attitude by businesses, non-profits, government agencies, and individuals that combining data from multiple sources could lead to better decisions.

However, in the whole area of big data there are tremendous opportunities for scouting and gaining insights beyond the normal business.

Of the numerous definitions, the last one is most applicable to the discussion in this chapter, the concrete scouting to gaining insights beyond the normal business.

Examples of possible new insights from big data

Folklore has it that the number of searches on Google is a good indicator for certain emerging health issues. For instance, as the searches on cold, fever, and so on increase in a certain demographic region, the outbreak of a flu epidemic may be better predicted this way, than through traditional methods. This insight may then provide the opportunity to bring enough relevant medicine to that region in time.

Likewise, scientific research is now indicating that, because changes in physical movements and behaviors in the early stages of diseases such as Alzheimer's take place well before any doctor will have seen the potential patient, they may be detected much earlier, through the analysis of mobile phone data. Now, in the context of the global mega-trend of aging populations, this may have some important implications, relevant both at the individual level and for societies and their health care systems as a whole.

In 2014 the topic of big data was moved along on the Gartner Hype Cycle from the "peak of inflated expectations" phase to "trough of disillusionment." Given all the different interpretations of big data, this may not be a surprise. However, there may also be some real technical, ethical, and regulatory issues. Potentially, especially in the light of aging populations and the associated health care issues, big data will move, *the whole area of big data is offering significant potential for scouting* at least in selected parts, into the "the slope of enlightenment" phase quite quickly. Therefore, the whole area of big data is offering significant potential for scouting, especially for looking beyond…

Scouting: Small Data – The Role of Anthropologists

Having briefly looked at the power of big data, let us turn to other scouting techniques that are deliberately focused on using a small number of samples.

Traditionally, these techniques are classified as qualitative market research techniques – as opposed to the quantitative approaches just discussed in the big data section. One of these traditional techniques is focus group discussion, for which a small group of say six to eight individuals is recruited for an in-depth discussion around a particular product or service. This is a very helpful technique to understand customers' needs in relation to existing products and services. It provides a good basis for exploitation.

Now, there is another level at which you can engage customers in innovation, the level of co-creation. In its simplest form a small number of customers are invited to take part in the organization's internal innovation workshops. Therefore, in addition to the normal market research reports and statistics, you now have real customers in the workshop to provide extra meaning to all the abstract data. At least for part of the innovation workshop you can then engage them in the pro-active idea generation process.

> ### BOX 6.2 CASE EXAMPLE: NEW YORK
>
> A financial services organization brought their top 30 people together for three days to refine their strategy for the Americas (North and South), including an agenda for innovation. The top team decided: We dare to bring in our New York clients, the brokers. For half a day seven brokers participated in this workshop.

New York brokers are known for many things, but not for being quiet and shy. They would not disappoint us. As uncomfortable as it may have been for the top 30 in the organization, they heard the clear messages directly. This is much more impactful than any market research report can ever be!

BOX 6.3 CASE EXAMPLE: GERMANY

We tried the same with a service organization in the more benign Germanic environment. The top 40 were assembled and we invited six key account customers to discuss innovation opportunities. Again that was an eye-opener, especially for the 20 or so people in charge of back-office functions. For some of them it was the first time they had met a real client!

Involving clients physically in innovation or strategy workshops for co-creation is a very powerful tool, as it brings all the abstract market research reports to life. Also, it demonstrates a level of trust to these clients, which is usually very much appreciated, and in fact creates a whole new customer experience.

These are examples of how small data can be used to very good effect for innovating in an organization. So, why should we not do more of that, if it works so well? The answer is simple – it works for exploitation; it does not work sufficiently for exploration, when looking beyond...

Here is the reason: In questionnaires, focus groups, or innovation workshops we are *asking* customers. There is nothing wrong with asking. However, what is the customers' reference point when answering? Yes, the existing products and services. Customers can most easily extrapolate from current products and services, so the answers we get are very helpful in exploitation, but generally quite poor in terms of discovering exploration opportunities.

The nature of the exploration challenge is to identify something that is beyond the current experience of the customers.
Therefore, it is difficult for them to articulate it.

There is an additional solution approach: Instead of asking, why not *observe* customers? The logic being, that if we accept customers are limited in the articulation of their ideas, then maybe, by observing them in depth, we can draw some conclusions for looking beyond.

Market research has a long tradition and experience in asking customers, but what about observation? Luckily here we can draw on the experience of about 100 years in a completely different scientific field, anthropology. According to Wikipedia:

> Anthropology as the study of humans, past and present, that draws and builds upon knowledge from the social sciences and biological sciences, as well as the humanities and the natural sciences.

As anthropology is covering a rather wide conceptual field, a special form of anthropology, called ethnography is of interest to our scouting discussion. Let us again turn to Wikipedia for a definition:

> Ethnography (from Greek ἔθνος ethnos "folk, people, nation" and γράφω grapho "I write") is the systematic study of people and cultures. It is designed to explore cultural phenomena where the researcher observes society from the point of view of the subject of the study. An ethnography is a means to represent graphically and in writing the culture of a group. An ethnography records all observed behavior and describes all symbol-meaning relations using concepts that avoid casual explanations.

The traditional role of anthropologists is to observe behavior in different cultures. This used to be very remote from any business activity. Today that has changed: Apparently, Intel is currently the largest employer of anthropologists, for example. Why? Anthropologists possess a key competence for exploring "shaping game" opportunities: Observation. In existing markets it is all about prediction, supported by traditional market research techniques. These traditional techniques will not let you develop the iPod, iPhone, or the iPad. However, the identification of patterns in the way individuals interact with the objects around them, such as with their car, will reveal opportunities way beyond the performance of the car or its design. On behalf of its customers Intel is investing heavily in observation as a source of new insights and exploration opportunities.

Following some initial individual applications of ethnography in organizations, since 2005 there is now a regular Ethnographic Praxis in Industry (EPIC) conference that focuses on the professional application of ethnography in the business context.

Ethnography does not capture what people say, but what they actually do. Now, the important part is that the observations are recorded and the observer does not interfere with the person being observed, therefore the observation is often also supported by video ethnography. It allows for fully understanding the context in which a customer is operating, rather than just focusing on the interactions related to specific products and services.

BOX 6.4 CASE EXAMPLE: INTEL

You may recall the point made in Chapter 1 about the car as a mobile data center. As a chip supplier to the car industry, Intel has quite an interest in and made a substantial contribution to this topic. Anthropologist Genevieve Bellan, director of user experience research at Intel Labs, provides an interesting example (Singer, 2014). As a response to ever more built-in technologies, Bellan wanted to find out how people shifted between the built-in technology and other personal devices. She and her team traveled to a number of countries and asked car users to empty their cars and placed the contents outside. What they found was that despite all the in-built devices, people were still carrying all sorts of personal devices with them, indicating that indeed the car as a mobile data center had not reached the messy day to day realities of people's lives.

These observations served as a reality check for Intel and its clients. Since then Intel has announced partnerships with Toyota and Jaguar Land Rover, in order to better synchronize the in-built devices with the mobile devices to avoid drivers having to reach out to their mobile devices whilst driving.

BOX 6.5 CASE EXAMPLE: INSURANCE

A few years back we sent out Polaroid cameras to selected private insurance clients of an insurance company. We asked them to take photographs of their interaction with the organization. What we got back were pictures of strewn papers on the kitchen table and of parents literally tearing their hair out. Now, these pictures vividly carried important messages. Innovation teams inside the organization were able to look at the current customer experience displayed, not just the normal market research statistics. This provided enormous triggers for figuring out ways of simplifying the customer experience.

Ethnography is using "small data" based on observation. Methodically, it should provide better insight for scouting and looking beyond traditional market research methods. Through observation, a more unbiased understanding of the real situation of a customer is achieved. Moreover, this observation is not just looking at the interaction with the products and services in question; it studies that interaction in the much wider context in terms of how customers lead their lives.

The Link to Design Thinking

The techniques developed within ethnography play an important part in the overall concept of design thinking, which has become an important, but academically controversial, concept in the field of innovation in recent years. How does this concept fit into ambidexterity, and in particular into the scouting discussion in this chapter?

Tom Kelley and Dave Kelley have over the years with their company IDEO pushed for the agenda of design thinking applications in the business context. In their most recent book (2013), design thinking has come to be defined as combining *empathy* for the context of a problem, *creativity* in the generation of insights and solutions, and *rationality* in analyzing and fitting various solutions to the problem context.

Empathy for the context refers to the methods of ethnography, the observational methods. Now, one important implication of using small data is the focus we apply to identifying the right customers to observe. Part of the design thinking architecture is to look at the extremes in order to do this. Along the normal distribution, the "bell curve," the interesting parts are at the extreme ends. For instance, the very heavy users vs the non-users; the very healthy vs the very sick. Ideation can then focus on very specific individuals in these extreme cases. By focusing on these it is quite likely that we will indeed be scouting, looking beyond!

Summary

This chapter has looked at a solution towards the ambidexterity challenge from the perspective of how to best scout the unknown territory for exploration.

In exploration, by definition, we cannot rely on predicting and forecasting. How can we establish the necessary data for shaping game strategies, for putting a stake in the ground?

The first part of the chapter looked at how organizations can perform the scouting activities under the purposeful strategic choice of being fast second. Some organizations focus on technology scouting, often guided by the Gartner Hype Cycle, in order to be alerted to how new technologies, such as the Internet of things, 3-D printing, and so on, can offer new opportunities.

Scouting functions are the organization's radar screen, which picks up technological developments early and builds appropriate initial relationships with start-ups. All this is done with a view to scaling these technological advances fast. However, the chapter also discussed the importance of political support for the scouting function within the company. If the technology scouting function is mainly used as a fig leaf to hide behind, then exploration in that organization will have a slim chance of prevailing.

The chapter went on to address the additional opportunities faced by organizations operating in a B2B2C environment. For these organizations, the beyond challenge includes the strategic beyond, in terms of "who is our customer?" Traditionally these organizations viewed their direct customers as the next in line of the value chain, the B-customer. Of course, you can already do a lot in terms of exploitation and exploration with the focus on that traditional, immediate customer. But what about going directly to the end-users, cutting out the middleman? This is a different level of exploration, as the organization usually has very little understanding of the end-user, compared to the very detailed understanding of the immediate B-customer.

New technology platforms make it feasible to establish a direct link with the end-user. The opportunity is often described as "Can we not be the Nespresso in our industry?" or "What is our equivalent to Intel inside?" Therefore, in order to address the appropriate solutions B2B2C organizations increasingly go beyond the normal B-customer in exploration projects to embrace the opportunities around the end-user. Scouting will then have to include purposefully understanding this end-user. This is often a completely new territory in which organizations have very little experience, because previously the "middle-man" has handled that relationship.

So how can we then understand the end-user? Surely one route must be applying "big data." How can we make sense of all the data that may be available in different data silos, from different sources? The answer currently is, with difficulty! Hence, the Gartner Group have moved the topic of big data to the category of "disillusionment." However, it would be wrong to pre-maturely write off big data as a source for looking beyond.

It may take a bit of time to identify smart ways of dealing with issues of data connectivity, public acceptance, regulatory approval, and development of some smart predictive modeling tools. It may be possible to apply big data approaches to address problems such as disease; for example, to identify the possible Alzheimer patient two years before any medical symptoms occur. In that case the individual, the health insurers, and societies determined by aging populations would benefit. It is inconceivable that the availability of so many potential benefits will not trigger smart solutions around the potential obstacles. Big data may have lost a bit of its shine, but it will remain a major source for scouting in years to come, whatever better name we may want to give it on the way.

From big data to small data: The chapter looked at the role of anthropology and its specific form, ethnography, which can bring us to a better understanding of the end-user. Ethnography documents people's behaviors in their natural context and analyzes their choice patterns. Ethnographers deploy advanced technologies that – remotely – track and visually record behaviors at home, work, and leisure.

Here the focus is on small data, in depth. Ethnography requires the focus to be on specific individuals. Identifying individual end-users is critical. It is usual to look at the opposite ends of the bell-curve, for instance the very healthy as opposed to the every sick.

Anthropology is becoming a key resource for organizations. Intel, for example, employs more than 50 anthropologists who continually study market opportunities, which they share with their customers. The free sharing of such market intelligence results in an alignment of R&D initiatives and shorter routes to market. In 2013 Intel published a whole book on the various aspects of ethnography (Salvador et al, 2013).

Understanding end-users is usually the starting point for the concept of design thinking. Empathy, creativity, and rationality are the building blocks of design thinking. These building blocks then will move us from a scouting beyond… to building very tangible new business concepts. Empathy is the detailed understanding of customers in their context, exactly the insight provided through ethnography.

In this chapter, scouting approaches that may help us to look beyond were discussed. The focus was primarily on the organizational implications. However, there are some implications for your own roles.

In your role as architect for ambidexterity:

Technology scouting: This is an important capability to install in your organization. In fact it is critical, if you have made the strategic choice to be fast second! However, make sure that the individuals in charge of technology scouting are not just technology experts. Their technical competencies should be purposefully augmented with being politically savvy and supported by a strong sponsor.

Customers: In a B2B2C setting you have the strategic opportunity of defining the end-user as "customer." If this is your strategic choice, then the question arises as to how you can get to a comfortable level of understanding with these customers.

Big data/small data: It is not either or, it is a clear and! How can you build up the processes and the capabilities to do both in a robust fashion?

In your role as project leader for an exploration project:

Technology scouting: Get in contact with your colleagues in technology scouting. They should quickly provide you with an overview of potentially relevant technologies – and possible concrete candidates for collaboration!

Customers: Sources, big data/small data – what do we already know? How can we cut both cost and time spent? Can we "piggy-back" on existing insights, possibly from other industries?

Extreme cases: Pick individual customers who may constitute an extreme case. This will ensure that you already start your project well in "beyond territory." Build your case, your story, around that extreme case.

chapter 7

Solution: Convergence Engineering

Why is this Important for You and for Your Organization?

Convergence between industries is happening all around us, as described in Chapter 1. However, just because it happens it does not mean we have, as individuals or as organizations a role to play. The benefits of convergence between industries are hard earned. Who assembles the right capabilities, the right partners, and the right formal set up? Both individuals and organizations have to earn the right to have a seat at the table, they have to clearly demonstrate their relevance.

This chapter will discuss what it takes for you individually and your organization to engineer to have a seat at the table. I have discussed this topic with many people in the last few years. Also, I have been privy to many confidential discussions, which for obvious reasons cannot be addressed here. However, I am fortunate to be able to draw on the experiences of four particular individuals whose ideas have influenced me significantly in recent years:

- Heidi Mason – the view from Silicon Valley and beyond.
- Christian Garbe – the view from biotechnology and beyond.

- Thomas Meyer – the view from financing/private equity and beyond.
- Roger Moser – the view from Asia and beyond.

In this chapter they will be offering their perspective on convergence engineering.

The chapter is organized in the following way: First it will look at the role of collaboration. Then it will address the need for engineering, the role of eco-systems, and the role of both mindset and vision. Finally, it will look at the role of corporate venturing and conclude with an example of convergence in the future of health care.

The Role of Collaboration

One aspect is clear; the benefits of convergence cannot be reaped without collaboration. At a minimum, this is collaboration inside the organization across functional units. However, many capabilities required are outside of the organization. Therefore, partnering, collaborating with other organizations, becomes a key organizational capability.

the benefits of convergence cannot be reaped without collaboration

Collaboration and partnering require a completely different leadership style compared to running a very focused own business. Inside the realms of the current business a lot can be achieved through telling and a transactional leadership style. However, this successful internal leadership style may result in the opposite effect in a collaborative environment.

Influencing without power is not a leadership style you acquire overnight. Chapter 3 discussed at length the importance of the T-Model for individual leaders. All the success factors in your personal leadership style, which brought you to the top of your functional career, may be questionable when it comes to leading cross-functional teams inside your

BOX 7.1 CASE EXAMPLE: DAIMLER BENZ AEROSPACE

When I joined in 1992, Daimler Benz had just acquired the majority of German aerospace interests. Now, the heritage of the Daimler Benz organization at the time was very much based on the Mercedes Benz car and truck tradition. Yes, as part of moving into aerospace there was a new strategy to develop an integrated technology company. Now, who were the people to implement that strategy? Of course, the individuals who successfully ran the Mercedes Benz car and truck divisions! At the time Mercedes Benz was a highly valued organization for its brand and technology achievements. As an organizational culture it was very much focused on the protection of this brand integrity. The cultural outcome was one very much dominated by a command and control leadership style, which at the time was also prevalent in many other German organizations.

As Daimler Benz then ventured into the aerospace industry, a whole new way of doing business awaited them. Instead of a full control over its car and truck value chain, the aerospace industry had a highly fragmented value chain. At the time, Daimler Benz controlled some 37.3 per cent of Airbus, as well as having involvement in activities such as the Ariane space project and in military projects such as the Eurofighter Daimler Benz. Now the precise, percentage figures do not matter. What matters is the fact that in Aerospace Daimler Benz had no majority in *any* of the businesses. Now what do leaders who have been groomed in a command and control environment do? Yes, they exercise command and control...

organization. However, the challenge gets amplified when you not only have to lead cross-functional but also cross-organizational, and worse still cross-industry, partnerships. At this point as a leader you are firmly in the territory of influencing without power.

Whether you are in the role of an architect, a project leader, or an implementer, you know that in a co-operation with other partners there will be no more "telling" other people what to do. Influencing – sometimes influencing without power – is the key to success.

Collaboration also has to be developed as an organizational capability. At the organizational level, how can we orchestrate influencing without power across your own organization and partner organizations? It obviously very much depends on the history of your organization. Some organizations may already have a history of managing joint venture activities; they will be quite advanced in collaboration as an organizational capability. Many organizations went through the process of outsourcing and will point out that they today can operate through a network of partners and suppliers. However, in these companies, especially when they are large, the outsourcing agreements will make it quite clear that the organization and not the partners will be in control.

If organizations want to take advantage of convergence opportunities in a proactive manner it is unlikely that they will be the lead partner in every convergence project engaged in. In fact they may have to learn to act in the role of a junior partner, when it is clear that an organization from a different industry should take the lead role on the basis that they may already have the most important capabilities assembled.

Collaboration as an organizational capability should cover the full spectrum of potential partnerships, ranging from being a junior partner to being clearly the lead partner. Influencing without power however, is required throughout that spectrum. Even if your organization is clearly the lead partner, you will still require the support from players in a different industry who may hold one of the critical capabilities for your project.

Dr. Thomas Meyer, partner at LDS Partners in Luxemburg and author and co-author of a number of books on the topic of private equity (Mathonet & Meyer, 2008; Meyer & Mathonet, 2011; Meyer, 2014), has kindly provided a historic perspective on collaboration in business. Meyer's focus is the development of risk measurement models and investment strategies for private equity funds, funds-of-funds, and institutional investment programs. Related to this, he has years of practical experience and has researched and published on public policy approaches to the development of venture capital markets.

BOX 7.2 THOMAS MEYER ON CONVERGENCE ENGINEERING

Persian traders, Medici

As a general comment I believe that we have a tendency to view innovation as result of an intellectual exercise. However, an alternative hypothesis is that ambidexterity is something that has "worked" throughout our history and as part of our "genetic" set-up and has long contributed to the growth and survival of our species. Innovation therefore – as a result of exploration – may be a (of course welcome) "side-effect" of human behavior rather than its end. For example, periods of long-term intensive warfare are often accompanied by bursts of technical innovation. The emergence of computers and telecommunication, Silicon Valley and the venture capital industry would most likely not have happened that rapidly without decades of military funding during two world wars and the Cold War. In this context innovation is a necessity to assure national survival; humans clearly do not engage in wars in order to stimulate innovation.

From the outset, I need to stress that I am not an anthropologist and my arguments regarding the exploitation part of ambidexterity are not researched and are my personal interpretation. My experience and the arguments in my books on private equity financing are centered around the limited partnership, which I view primarily as an organizational form for exploration, i.e., the vehicle to "boldly go where no man has gone before".

My main point is that repeatedly in history humans invented and reinvented the limited partnership and very similar structures to solve the same combination of problems: investments under high uncertainty, where opportunities only exist temporarily and the payoff potentially is enormous, but not really quantifiable.

Why should exploration be externally managed?

Private equity funds resemble, for instance, the commenda contract for trade voyages that is widely credited as having contributed to Venice's riches in medieval times. While "exploration" appears to be mainly done by individuals and small organizations – such as nimble ship crews – the task of "exploitation" calls for more lasting and larger organizations with efficient infrastructure and the associated bureaucracies. In his 1995 book *Trust* Francis Fukuyama argues that social capital is as important as physical capital and that only societies with a high degree of social trust are able to create large-scale organizations that can operate globally. He viewed, for illustration, Italy and China as societies where there is little trust in managerial talent outside one's own family and, as a consequence, firms find it difficult to grow internationally. Fukuyama did not specifically touch upon the aspect of loyalty, but most large organizations are held together by a selected group of top managers. Here loyalty to the CEO, the corporate culture, its products and production processes etc. is probably even more critical than competence, and innovation is rather a threat to the stability of these organizations and even raises the suspicion of being disloyal.

In this respect the modern companies could be argued to resemble medieval kingdoms and, in fact, the relationships between top managers in all economies look in many ways like the family ties of old nobility. The price for the ability to administrate "empires where the sun never sets" through a loyal group of confidants is the downside of loyalty, such as groupthink and the rejection of outsiders and new ideas. Probably most humans prefer enjoying safety, high status and the associated wealth in larger organizations, but unfortunately only a selected few will succeed in climbing the greasy pole and become member of the "nobility" running these companies. Of course, larger organizations are also innovating, but only in a comparatively incremental way which is not viewed as "disloyal" and mainly through adaptation. No significant innovation will happen without consensus being achieved among the top management team, based on thorough analysis and backed up by a lot of data. Such organizations are not risk averse, but only risk of the uncontroversial kind is taken on and only if not threatening to the company's overall position.

"Breakthrough" innovation is, by definition, about the "unknown unknowns" and about going against conventional wisdom and any consensus. A number of researchers are suspecting an "explorer gene" that drives innovators to go their own way. An alternative (simpler and more sobering) explanation in many cases could lie in the human behavioral trait to bully individuals that do not conform and force or frustrate (e.g., companies denying recognition and promotions) them out of the tribe – essentially forcing them to become explorers.

Logic for collaboration, reality of big egos

GM, Apple, Microsoft and Sony at one time in their history were all considered to be firms with highly innovative products that also embraced innovations as organizations and underwent, occasionally drastic, shifts in strategy. But at the time such innovations appear to have been driven top down: it is difficult to see that even in these firms innovations would have happened without their powerful and charismatic "kings" – leaders like Jack Welch, Steve Jobs, Bill Gates and Akio Morita. Would these firms also have reached a consensus for ideas conceived by lower echelons in the organizations and then "floated" bottom-up? For Steve Jobs it is reported that he often took ideas from others but only after he had convinced himself (and the rest of the world) that these ideas were his in the first place. I am therefore skeptical regarding the existence of ambidextrous companies, at least not over the long term; it is more ambidexterity in industries and alliances between companies that appears to allow blending of the two contrarian modes of exploration and exploitation in a value-creating way.

Lessons learned from a historical perspective

The limited partnerships used by the private equity industry are often viewed as an early 20th century invention, but this style of investing goes back thousands of years. Comparable trade partnerships were already common in early Babylonia. So what strikes me is how little the various forms of cooperation between humans actually have changed. Designing new forms of collaboration, in my eyes, is bound to fail without considering the often 'dark side' of human traits and taking lessons from history into account.

Thomas Meyer, December 2014

Why Engineering?

Here is a personal case: Two years ago I worked in the space of two months with six companies from six different industries. In all these top management meetings the focus was on how to create an agenda 2018/20 given the mega-trends around us. The fascinating insight for me was that everyone was addressing very similar opportunities. However, all my clients were naturally addressing those opportunities from their own vantage points. Everyone realized that they had to do "innovation beyond the current industry boundaries" and that additional corporate capabilities were required. The identification of what these capabilities actually were, and where and how to get them, created a big puzzle.

At that point I realized the need for engineering, the purposeful connection between partners across industries.

Dr. Christian Garbe has been the CEO of FiZ since 2002. The FiZ Frankfurt Biotechnology Innovation Center is a market-oriented technology center, which offers small and medium-sized companies in the life sciences sector a customized infrastructure for innovations with access to collaborations, interdisciplinary networks, and markets. Garbe oversees expansion in physical space and supports the global expansion of the FiZ companies. He held numerous workshops and instigated a number of collaborative ventures in order, he says, to initiate new business models and to develop "New German Engineering" for the life science sector.

BOX 7.3 INTERVIEW WITH DR. CHRISTIAN GARBE OF FIZ

Why the personal passion?

I'm actually a farmer with a Ph.D. in institutional economics. Therefore, I always seek recipes to minimize the target failure costs. I worked for Novartis and as a biotechanalyst in the financial sector. Clients say I'm passionate and always think outside the usual boxes. But that's exactly the craziness that robust, competitive business models require today. It's really a personal passion for me: New German engineering. Or, in other words, convergence engineering!

What is your experience around convergence:

- **What works?**
- **Are there any patterns?**

Certainly I haven't found the universal world formula yet. But after nearly 50 years of job and life experience, four success factors in business engineering are crucial for me, especially for the life science sector:

1) Life science focus: System diseases – and these are in fact the major diseases – can only be treated systemically. The old model of "one pill fits all" does not work anymore. The ancient knew: No effect without side effects and every person is different.

2) Business focus: The most robust business models are system models. To respond to increasing pressure with regard to costs and competition, companies are focusing more and more on efficient process and transfer innovations and no longer merely on research intensive and costly technologies. That means: Today you need smart and unique combinations of very complex value drivers (chain partners, your intellectual property, HR...). Research and value-added chains combine world-wide partner networks to satisfy global and local market needs.

3) Biotech + business: It is always easier said than done: These system approaches must be combined. This is also the reason why venture investors evaluate mainly the quality of the teams: the future is always uncertain. The sales forecasts are just estimates only. Therefore, an investor has only two assets – more or less: Is this team really complementary and can it solve complex challenges? What is their robust IP – how smart is the DNA of the business model?

4) Interfaces and synergies are crucial: Today innovations occur at the interfaces of the sciences. A campus structure alone is no guarantee for conversions. However, synergies won't come alone – you have to find and moderate them!

What does not work? Are there any patterns?

Strategies are increasingly interchangeable. Because all of them follow the same mega-trends. Indeed, these plans always seem to be perfect. They look smart and beautiful but are risky fata morganas because markets are always tricky and complex. Therefore, I plead for a business engineering approach: Even business models should be developed with engineering passion and perfection!

What matters most is a genuine culture and an environment in which such systems approaches are put into practice. This requires employees who want to build bridges. The FiZ management calls this: Building bridges from biology to business.

What matters most is a genuine culture

It's not so much about perfect plans. It is important to enable and to organize skills! Large companies fail because they design jobs like screws. And they wonder: The work has been divided to the maximum, a lot of smart experts are on board and many, many project managers have to moderate them. At the end, everything has become too fat for fast, relevant, and robust innovations.

Any concrete case examples you can share?
Apple is good at making a perfect combination of software and hardware. For example, chief creative Jonathan Ive is responsible for the hardware and for the screen design. Also, Apple has always remained watchful for new patents and technologies – behind the scenes, of course. Thus, they secure options for new, very smart combinations. Last but not least Apple became, in another crucial step, a networker for the content industry with very robust and powerful contracts – the same yet with mobile payment. It needs an inspired company with employees who are more than just experts in their own silo. Nokia has missed an opportunity of providing perfect software. If you're really obsessed with what you are doing, you can think of many steps further.

On the FiZ campus, we build on a very promising start-up, which will be a decision enabler for the entire life science industry. We call it Creating Superior Insights – CSI/X. We think further – for the next five to ten years: How will the business model spread? How do we become a strong industry standard? If you want to reach for the stars, you have to think further and wider! As simple and as complex as that!

Eco-System: Awareness, Access, Action

When it comes to the topic of innovation, the concept of an eco-system is never far away. Now, in ambidexterity, in particular in exploration activities, the case for collaboration, inside the organization, the industry, and beyond the industry has already been established.

Moore (1996) defined "business ecosystem" as follows:

> An economic community supported by a foundation of interacting organizations and individuals – the organisms of the business world. The economic community produces goods and services of value to customers, who are themselves members of the ecosystem. The member organisms also include suppliers, lead producers, competitors, and other stakeholders. Over time, they coevolve their capabilities and roles, and tend to align themselves with the directions set by one or more central companies. Those companies holding leadership roles may change over time, but the function of ecosystem leader is valued by the community because it enables members to move toward shared visions to align their investments, and to find mutually supportive roles.

Convergence engineering is supported through extending existing or building new eco-systems. Silicon Valley is probably the most prominent example of a highly effective eco system. However, eco-systems are not always based on close geographic proximity. Especially, when experimenting with a new shaping game opportunity, the "home" market may turn out to be the worst starting point. There is too much at stake, the public opinion, and the regulators. "Where does a snowball start to melt?" This is the question I always heard from C. K. Prahald when he wanted to remind me of the fact, that real innovation is taking place in a low-risk environment, under the radar screen. Of course, the snowball does not melt from within; having lived in Switzerland for more than 15 years I have enough practical evidence that the snowball indeed melts from the outside! An eco-system has to reflect that. Therefore, an eco-system has to go beyond Silicon Valley. It needs to be connected to the hotspots around the world. An early example of that is the fact that the now ubiquitous Red Bull drink was first invented in Thailand as a method of keeping truck drivers alert on their long cross-country journeys.

Prof. Dr. Roger Moser leads the Asia Connect Center (ACC) at the University of St. Gallen. He is also adjunct professor at the Indian Institute of Management Udaipur.

BOX 7.4 AN INTERVIEW WITH PROF. DR. ROGER MOSER OF THE ACC

At the ACC you are dealing with inbound and outbound connections covering countries such as India, China, Singapore, and Thailand. What are the driving forces for organizations seeking out the ACC connections?

The ACC supports companies from Asia as well as Europe during their market entry and expansion activities in the other continents. Both European and Asian companies face the primary challenge of access to local industry intelligence as well as local decision makers. The ACC at the University of St. Gallen and its academic partners in Asia serve as neutral platforms for companies to better investigate how their business models need to look in a different institutional context and to identify potential business partners for the implementation.

Increasingly, the business models that these companies develop are not based on integrated develop–produce–sell activity chains but rather, for example, on access-based solutions. This requires the companies not only to think in completely new ways of collaboration re-defining their own roles and those of their business partners but also to interact with new partners from industries that have traditionally no connection to their own sector. For example, high-end Japanese, German, or Swiss sewing machines can easily cost 3,000–5,000 CHF. Given the social and cultural background of India there are only relatively few people who are able and willing to buy such a machine. In fact, most of those who are able might not be willing (e.g. members of high-income families) and those who might be willing are not always able (e.g. young textile designers). As a result, the market potential for high-end sewing machines in India seems very limited. However, if we try to offer a solution for those who are willing but not able to purchase a high-end sewing we might still identify an interesting market in India.

Such a focus requires that a company turns away from the classic develop–produce–sell model and instead tries to provide potential customers with access to their products only when they really need it and at a price that they can afford. In our example, this requires that a) the target customers (e.g. young designers) have convenient access and b) that the utilization rate of the machine is high enough to offer a price per hour of usage that the target customer can afford. The solution that we developed jointly with such a high-end sewing machine included a collaboration with a national coffee shop chain to establish "creative corners" in coffee shops close to design institutes where students could hang-out, develop new designs, and try them in "real time" using the high-end sewing machines on an hourly basis.

However, such access-based business models often require senior executives to develop relationships with business partners that they are not used to dealing with (e.g. coffee shop chains or design schools) and the development of local networks with unusual stakeholders as well as a different and more detailed understanding of customer requirements. This is a form of convergence thinking that I believe offers new opportunities for those companies that know how to engineer and implement such new collaborations.

How are the activities related to actively fostering/engineering convergence?

Based on my experience with MNCs as well SMEs it is primarily the mindset of the senior executives that is decisive of whether a company proactively fosters convergence thinking and provides the necessary resources to engineer convergence-based solutions. In general, the more experience senior executives have with new markets (Europe and Asia respectively) the better they understand that the different institutional contexts require radically different solutions. Once this mindset has been established, they are very much open to developing solutions based on proactive convergence engineering.

Are there specific experiences/differences in the partnerships between:

- **Small and large organizations?**
- **Large and large organizations?**

Interestingly, it is mostly the large companies that are most reluctant to get engaged in unusual collaborations based on proactive convergence engineering. Even more so, large companies are more cautious to get engaged with small organizations as compared to other large companies.

Does convergence depend on pro-active engineering? Does it not happen automatically in times of Google et al?

We at ACC are organizing different convergence platforms in Asia – for Western as well as Asian companies. There is not a single convergence between industries or companies happening automatically, because it is not about technology but mindset and innovation. Without experts and neutral platforms I can hardly imagine how companies openly exchange ideas or identify all necessary partners.

Looking into the future: Any expectations on how convergence engineering will develop?

The next five to seven years will bring a massive mindset change. An increasing number of executives understand already that the fastest growing companies and their underlying business logic cannot be explained (anymore) without an understanding of the convergence of industries. When customers do not ask for products or services anymore that they have to combine on their own but integrated solutions offering convenience and cost advantages, companies will be forced to implement convergence engineering in the future similar to how they do strategic planning today.

Vision/Mindset from Individual Perspectives

Each participant in shaping game strategies will have their own perspective, their "own picture," their own vision. However, over and beyond their own vision, in collaboration they subsequently have to create a joint picture, which still reflects their individual perspective.

Who is the target audience for a vision? A vision is aimed at creating alignment inside the organization. This is critical, as in shaping game strategies we are moving away from the core business, the core capabilities. A vision is therefore important to create the permission and support from the top as well as creating the buy-in from other functional stakeholders inside the organization. The vision should also be strong enough to win over the partners from other organizations, with whom you need to collaborate.

A vision should also create a link between the achievements of the past, the now, including the urgency for action, and an exciting picture of the future. The own vision is very much determined by four factors:

1) Orthodoxies. The dominant logic, the historic DNA code of the organization (and often of a whole industry). The mindsets – the orthodoxies – pull back companies like a magnet. They reinforce the core-competencies. Here we are safe; we are in known territory.
2) The benefits. The potential rewards such as new revenue streams, higher margins, and new levels of competitiveness. This is the upside view of creating a sense of urgency.
3) The enemies. Here it is not so much the known competitors but the disrupters who can come in from a different industry and threaten the core business. This is looking at the downside to create a sense of urgency.
4) Missing capabilities. Each player is the owner of certain capabilities; each player in the new game also misses certain pieces of the puzzle.

A joint vision among the collaboration partners is providing the glue to keep the partnership going, especially in phases which may be dominated by technological challenges and various forms of resistance.

Corporate Venturing

When investigating the approaches to convergence engineering, we also have to look at the role of "corporate venturing" as another way in which corporations participate in global innovation and new venture development to ensure strategic expansion and long-term growth. University of California Berkeley Business School professor Henry Chesbrough developed the paradigm of "open innovation." This observes that companies benefit from external ideas, as well as their own internal strengths and ideas, and asserts that the combination of these internal and external paths to market accelerates technology and innovation acceptance and commercial growth. "Corporate venturing" (CV) is the operationalization of these ideas; corporate venture capital (CVC) programs, in particular, help organizations in accessing external innovation, playing a role in the development of innovation and new business models for growth on a global scale. These CVC programs typically focus on technologies and new markets adjacent but distinct from the company's core businesses. CVC teams require a degree of organizational autonomy in order to effectively blend corporate and new venture investment and development.

Heidi Mason (2011), in her landmark article, summarizes the 50-year-old history of corporate venturing by identifying five waves, which seem to be associated with the ups and downs of the business cycle:

Wave 1: In the 1960s some 25 per cent of Fortune 500 established Corporate Venture Units (CVUs). This wave lasted until the early 1970s.

Wave 2: Starting in the late 1970s fuelled by tax changes; especially high tech and pharmaceutical companies participated. This wave lasted until the stock-market crash in 1987.

Wave 3: The dot com era until 2000.

Wave 4: 2006–8 saw a short wave, very much curtailed by the financial crisis in 2008.

Wave 5: Since 2011 there has been a shift from vertical to horizontal thinking, internal innovation networks linking to external eco-systems, and performance measurement becoming more sophisticated.

The first four waves described by Mason focus on the vertical: How a company can outperform within its industry. The fifth wave includes some significant implications for horizontal innovation: The convergence between industries.

BOX 7.5 INTERVIEW WITH HEIDI MASON

Heidi Mason is a veteran of Silicon Valley and co-founder and managing partner of the Bell Mason Group (BMG), a specialty consultancy serving global corporations that seek strategic growth through corporate venturing and innovation (CV&I) initiatives. Mason serves as a strategic advisor to Global 1000 corporations that are focused on innovation, new markets, and new business creation through venturing. I asked her how she saw the role of corporate venturing today, especially in the context of convergence and its potential for convergence engineering.

What happened after you wrote the article in 2011?

In fact, significant changes happened: More than half of the current corporate venture units were formed after 2009. There has been significant growth in the level of activity. The organization Global Corporate Venturing has been monitoring the level of investment activity for many years. In 2014 they detected a record level of global deal activities through broadening corporate investment syndicates and collaborations. The change has been significant. The drive towards horizontal innovation (convergence) is much more pronounced than we anticipated.

What were the drivers for this shift?

The need for growth! Following the financial crisis, organizations were under enormous pressure to identify growth opportunities in an uncertain macro economy. This pressure led to a fresher thinking and to the acceptance that thinking beyond industry boundaries was required. At the same time, organizations such as Google and Amazon showed how they can take existing industries up to a new level, without the constraints of legacy businesses. The threat of these new disrupters galvanized many incumbents into action.

Are we still on the fifth wave?

Looking back at the 50-year-long history of corporate venturing, I think we are now in the middle of a tectonic shift. In today's context, the relatively incremental progress, which we have described as waves, is no longer adequate to characterize today's environment.

What constitutes this tectonic shift to a new generation: What is different this time?

The landscape is changing in fundamental ways, and these changes are literally reshaping industries:

1) Ubiquitous technology: Mobile, cloud, social media, Internet of everything – the "perfect storm" affects every business everywhere on the planet. This has led to collapsed development times and a necessarily faster cadence for innovation.

2) Horizontal thinking is now required. Vertical or functional silos are now understood to be counterproductive and that connecting partners across eco-systems is necessary. These new competitors have no such structural limitations.

3) Customer-centric solutions: Ubiquitous technology means that increasingly end-to-end solutions are possible, and when possible, are superior.

We have identified three key pivot points for a new era of CVC:

1) Time compression: Three-year timescale is the necessary new norm in which to demonstrate meaningful progress inside a global corporation as outside in the global marketplace. This is a significant reduction from the previously accepted innovation time frame of five years plus. Internally, this time scale reduction is compounded by what seems to be the natural tenure of corporate executives in positions and typical cycles of corporate reorganizations (also three years). If progress isn't seen within the three previous years, the new corporate

executive/successor with responsibility for CVC will probably start all over again, or at the very least, interrupt the current operation and slow its momentum – often enough to lose competitive positioning and deal access in the external world.

2) Next generation CVC "power tools" – beating the clock:

a) **Eco-system mapping:** This frames investment focus areas and connects portfolio strategy to a map for its execution – CVC eco-system mapping is challenging and time consuming to do well, but those who are doing it, are also accelerating their performance against their goals. End-to-end eco-system models "deconstruct" how local-to-global eco-systems operate, creating a picture of how their key elements and players interrelate and connect. This provides a frame for the CVC team to identify a system of focal points for investment and develop a cogent "make-minority invest-buy-partner" strategy to drive integrated portfolio development (convergence). This CVC eco-mapping technique helps teams turn their strategic portfolio investment map into impactful types of strategic and financial value return, faster.

b) **CVC "market-maker" investment tools:** Many groups' charters are expanding beyond individual minority investments, and are now including active engagement with M&A, growth PE, and other means of quickly building "roll-ups" and collaboration among their portfolio companies (another type of convergence of previously separate tools adapted as continuous CVC tool suite). The benefit for all is instant leverage points among portfolio companies and other types of identified partners, ensuring "embedded" strategic and financial "multipliers" and portfolio position for each of its investments. Other forms of innovation business and technology partnering are also now converging in CVC programs, "connecting the dots" with other corporate innovation mechanisms and groups that handle strategic alliances, R&D, IP & licensing, M&A, joint ventures and joint development, commercial piloting and incubators, and so on.

3) CV team and compensation: The key to recruiting, retention, and – finally – institutionalization of CV as a mainstream, corporate innovation function and contributor to long-term corporate growth:

   a) CVC compensation structures are the test of the corporation's intentions and its ability to effectively compete for the "right" senior level team members with the required mix of specialized skills – and ensure they stay together. CVC teams require a unique blend of specialized skills that complement one another and are rarely found complete in one individual. Ambidextrous organizational principles and convergence thinking are now critical to building the right type of teams of individuals whose specialized skills mesh to bridge the corporate and venture worlds.

   b) CVC compensation structures are the ultimate test of corporate "seriousness" on this topic. A position in a CV unit must be seen as a beneficial career move within the corporation, with rational risk/reward compensation structures and performance expectations, along with a formal path for succession planning. Otherwise, CV positions at the corporation are really a limitation for an individual who is high performance and career oriented – the CVC role instead becomes functional training, professional development on the way to another more respected and impactful operating job, and ensuring a revolving door of CVC candidates and team members of variable qualifications. In these cases, the loss of program momentum and ability to deliver performance is inevitable, along with the loss of institutional knowledge that comes and goes with individuals not incented to stay and build the CVC program and team.

Can you provide examples of good convergence engineering?
In today's high-urgency, rapidly moving world it can no longer be just about individual deals, or even about a portfolio, and the solutions depend on converged, systems engineering. This is required if the results are to be sustaining.

Global Health Innovation (GHI), the CVC group set up by Merck in 2010 is a good example. GHI's leader and team are emblematic of the new era of CVC. Their portfolio strategy and significant value return to date is driven by their eco-system vision, expanded suite of CVC "market maker" tools and its leader's assembly of the right CVC team. For example, GHI portfolio company Preventice, a remote patient care system, combines the knowledge and leverage of the pharmaceutical company Merck and that of the Mayo Clinic. Under GHI's stewardship, Preventice has merged with another of GHI's portfolio companies in remote monitoring, eCardio, which was also backed by Sequoia, a top tier Silicon Valley VC firm. Combined, they accelerate GHI and Merck's influence in the fast growing remote monitoring market with an "anchor" position in GHI's portfolio, building a powerful platform to drive innovation and accelerated market growth in the next stage of the health care industry.

In agriculture, Monsanto has been pushing the boundaries in augmenting their key capabilities around seed with climate information and on pest control, which has led to significant increases in soil yields. The benefits of these successful convergence engineering efforts by Monsanto Growth Ventures will be felt globally.

CitiVentures, the integrated internal innovation and external investment arm of Citi, is also leading the way for the "future of banking," embodying CVC attributes and portfolio strategy in areas of mobile-cloud, big data/analytics, cyber security, virtual currency, and has worked closely with the Silicon Valley eco-system, partnering for investment in innovative companies like Square.

The role of eco-systems: You have been based in Silicon Valley, which in itself has been praised as being the prime example of a successful eco-system. In terms of convergence engineering even Silicon Valley may be too small an eco-system. How will the role of eco-systems develop?

Here is where eco-system mapping comes in. Eco-systems have to be seen from an end-end perspective and the global eco-system needs to be supported by local eco-systems.

Eco-systems come from a blend of entrepreneurial infrastructure and insight with the implications of global, interconnected markets. The entrepreneurial "best practices" unquestionably originated in areas like Silicon Valley. Its unique eco-system is the high performance "engine" behind its historical success, which has led others in other areas around the world to strive to replicate and adapt the SV model in their local environments.

Understanding the dynamics and unique skills of local players and local environments that comprise these international innovation hubs – and how local players connect end-to-end – becomes critical to understanding how to succeed for local collaboration. At the same time, localized innovation eco-understanding converges at a larger, global level in a vision and "system" strategy for how to connect to one another at a global level – leading the way as to how to effectively maneuver and connect elements across these hubs and eco-systems from a local to global level, to accelerate CVC programs, portfolio and investment development, corporate value delivery, and the corporation's emerging market impact and influence.

As we have all progressively understood, especially in the last five years with the explosion of technologies and access that instantly connects and enables us all, "local" is not enough to be successful in today's world. In addition to global corporations with business infrastructures established around the world, new ventures must have a global outlook from their birth. Innovation hubs in other parts of the world are now critical to new ventures that form in them, providing a local environment with a better perspective on the necessities, demands, and opportunities for global strategies and market development.

Convergence – the Future of Health Care

When discussing convergence in this book we have frequently looked at the mega-trend aging population as a key driver for convergence in general. In the final section of this chapter it is worth highlighting that the future of health care provides a major focal point for convergence.

The convergence is not so much driven by the organizations participating in this sector but by individuals around the globe. Heidi Mason identified the impact of ubiquitous technology on organizations and the same can be said for individuals around the globe. Figure 7.1 illustrates this impact of technology developments on the way an individual can utilize different sets of technologies to improve personal health.

The individual, the segment of one is triggered by some event, for example, diagnosis of an illness or, at the other extreme, the decision to run a marathon.

Individuals today have the opportunity to have their DNA code analyzed at a cost of some US$60 in the US or €300 in Europe. The fact is that the cost for a DNA analysis has come down so much so that it is now within reach for a much larger part of the population. At the time of writing, however, the majority of the population does not yet take this up. In fact at this

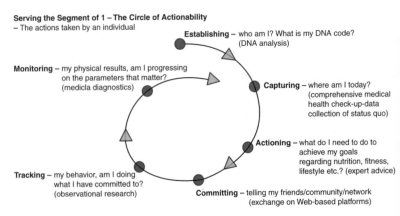

FIGURE 7.1 The Circle of Actionability

stage it is individuals at the extreme ends of the health spectrum, the very ill and the very healthy, who are utilizing it. The very ill can benefit from a DNA analysis by running their DNA results against a "pharma sensor." This helps them to identify which elements of a given drug cocktail are possibly harmful to them. At the other extreme, a person who is training for a triathlon, marathon, or climbing an extreme mountain is highly motivated to understand better how, based on their understanding of the DNA code, they should train and how they should adjust their nutritional habits.

With the DNA analysis individuals have established a baseline. This information can easily be augmented by a comprehensive medical check-up. This check-up would identify the baseline across a number of key medical parameters. The new elements of technology allow for this check-up to be done in a mobile fashion, where the doctor with his/her diagnostic kit can come to the home or the office of the individual. Next to an interpretation of the medical findings, the doctor will also put the results of the DNA analysis into perspective. However, the most important element to put the individual in charge of is data ownership. The data established through both DNA and medical analysis can be put together, allowing the individual to understand and have access to a comprehensive set of relevant health data. With this baseline established, it is then possible to develop targets for specific health parameters through the following phases:

1) **Actioning** triggers a whole array of possible activities related to specific fitness activities, changes in nutritional habits, and general lifestyle.
2) **Committing** this then uses the power of social networks to make commitments to friends and family regarding the actions decided upon. Likewise, new communities of like-minded action takers provide re-enforcement.
3) **Tracking** provides a follow-up on the commitments made. Here, the experiences with wristbands for example, come in: Has the individual actually taken the 7,000 steps today?
4) **Monitoring**. At this stage concrete measures are being taken: Have the health parameters identified actually been changed? How can gaps still existing be closed? What are the new targets? At this stage the circle of actionability is starting again, allowing the individual to be in charge of his/her own health.

Now, if these elements of the circle of actionability can be identified from the perspective of an individual, there will be the following implications for organizations trying to support this individual:

- Deciphering his/her DNA code (DNA analysis).
- Professional advice on changes in lifestyle, nutritional habits, fitness, and so on (thorough medical advice).
- Finding the appropriate resources (Web-based support).
- Monitoring the change in actual behavior (observational research).
- Diagnosing key health parameters (medical diagnostics).
- Revision/adaptation of the action plan (based on medical advice).

A number of different capabilities have to be aligned to fully take advantage of the new opportunities presented:

- Rapid prototyping.
- Observational market research.
- Diagnosis of medical conditions.
- Provision of medical advice.
- Provision of nutritional advice.
- Design of individual training/fitness programs.
- Data management – providing access when it matters.
- Managing collaborative partnerships.

Why is this a driver for convergence? Why is engineering important?

From the perspective of the individual, each stage of the circle of actionability offers a plethora of choices:

each stage of the circle of actionability offers a plethora of choices

- Which DNA analyses should I take?
- Which doctor should I trust to do the medical analysis?
- Whose advice on fitness, nutrition, and lifestyle should I trust?
- How do I avoid contradictory advice?

- Which apps should I trust?
- How can I come up with a consistent way of managing my health and well-being?

The various capabilities rest today in different industries. As individuals may want to address their health more from a holistic perspective, the more pressure there will be for organizations from different industries to augment their specific capabilities with that of partners from different industries.

Summary

This chapter has looked at convergence and the need for engineering to take advantage of the opportunities presented through convergence.

The need for collaboration

Convergence between industries and the associated exploration projects requires collaboration between different functions, organizations, and even industries. "Influencing" therefore becomes both a critical organizational capability as well as a key competence required by the individuals acting on behalf of these organizations. In his contribution to this chapter, Thomas Meyer offered an interesting historic perspective. Private equity partnerships as we know them today are in fact based on patterns of collaboration in exploration projects well established for centuries. Therefore, as today we are looking at convergence engineering, a lot can be learned from the experience of running limited partnerships as the backbone of private equity investments. In exploration projects trust and firm agreements on roles and responsibilities matter. This includes robust agreements on splitting the outcomes of fruitful exploration projects.

The need for engineering

Opportunities for convergence may be blatantly obvious. However, for convergence to happen it seems to require a catalyst, a platform to trigger the launch of exploration projects between different partners. Christian Garbe in his interview pointed out that systems thinking drives the future of health care, and biotech in particular. Using the German engineering tradition as a benchmark, he postulates the same level of professionalism in managing system partnerships between relevant partners across industries. This need for "engineering" was very much echoed by the interviews with both Roger Moser and Heidi Mason. Roger Moser pointed out the role of a purposefully created eco-system. Heidi Mason highlighted the role of internal corporate venture units to purposefully engineer convergence.

The role of eco-systems

Roger Moser, in his interview, pointed out the need for eco-systems to provide a platform from which to purposefully launch exploration projects. These eco-systems should not just be spanning across geographies, but also across industries. Heidi Mason even focused on purposeful eco-system mapping as a key organizational capability in order to take full advantage of both local and global eco-systems.

The role of a vision in convergence engineering

To run exploration projects in the space of industry convergence is indeed very challenging. As we are in unchartered territory, we will encounter all sorts of unexpected surprises and set-backs; hence the more important it is that for these exploration projects we have a robust vision that can act as a goal post or a lighthouse to keep the exploration project on track. The creation of a jointly shared vision is an important corner stone for convergence engineering.

The role of corporate venturing

Organizations increasingly use purposefully internal "corporate venture" units (CVUs) to facilitate the engineering of convergence opportunities. As Heidi Mason in her contribution describes, these CVUs have increasingly moved their focus from a traditional vertical (industry) focus to a horizontal (convergence) one. By doing so these CVUs have the potential to become the engineers to facilitate exploration projects, utilizing well orchestrated local and global eco-systems.

The role of customer-centric solutions

The perfect storm Heidi Mason described around ubiquitous technology (mobile, cloud, social media, Internet of everything) has one clear winner – the individual. Individuals around the globe now have access to resources in an unprecedented manner. Each smartphone in operation today is customized already through the specific utilization of apps and so on. The customers are therefore getting accustomed to the fact that they can individualize, that they can have their unique, individual service. In marketing terms, we can call this the emergence of the "segment of one".

In the example around health care it was demonstrated that the circle of actionability is leading to very individualized requirements. This will require customer-centric solutions from organizations that want to participate in this mega trend. In a way, from a customer's perspective, "the genie is out of the bottle." The notion of the segment of one is here to stay and will prove to be a major driver for convergence, and the need for convergence engineering.

What are the implications for your organization?

How can your organization get a seat at the table?

Awareness: Is the organization and with it the key decision makers aware of both the opportunities and dangers of convergence?

Collaboration: What is the organization's experience and track record around collaboration?

Eco-systems: Is there an awareness of and access to global and/or local eco-systems?

Vision: Does the organization offer a "point of view," a "vision" that can establish itself as a pivotal player to orchestrate eco-systems beyond industry boundaries?

Organization: Are there clear roles and responsibilities around the opportunities and dangers of convergence?

Customer-centric: Does the organization have the capacity to customize and to build meaningful long-term relationships with customers?

What are the implications for you as an individual?

How can you get a seat at the table?

Awareness: Are you in the "loop" regarding convergence in your industry/your function?

Visibility: Do people inside/outside of your organization value your input/opinion regarding convergence? To what extent are you positioned as a thought leader?

Influencing: To what extent are you comfortable in an environment which can be described as influencing without power? Does that differ between your own organization and potential partner organizations?

Patience: To what extent are you prepared and/or able to exercise patience – with your own organization and partner organizations?

There may also be some specific aspects according to your role. As an architect: How do you organize for exploration to deal with convergence? What is your vision for taking advantage of convergence opportunities? How do you incentivize people in exploration projects? What kind of HR processes need to be in place to build and maintain an exploration infrastructure?

As a project leader: How can you keep momentum in motivating other partners, inside and/or outside your own organization? How should you manage key stakeholders and sponsors?

8

Solution De-risking: Creating Robust Organizational Architectures

---

Why is this Important for You and for Your Organization?

Risk is the common denominator between the individual and the organization. How much personal risk in terms of your own career are you prepared to accept? Is the level of risk supported by the organization and how can you deal with it? At the same time the organization wants to create the future with minimum risk, of course. Here the question is: Are we avoiding risk or are we managing risk? How can the organization put a robust architecture in place, which mitigates the risk for both the individual and the organization?

This chapter will identify the key elements of risk. Then three case examples will be used to illustrate how the risk for both individual and organization can be reduced. Finally, the chapter will draw some general conclusions and recommendations for de-risking.

Nature of Risk: Individual/Organizational Levels

Any innovation activity carries risks: At the personal level, it is the reputational risk especially in a zero-defect organization. Support through a sponsor and a robust exploration process are critical to de-risking personal risk for the individual.

At the organizational level, the market risks, technology risks, and reputational risks need to be addressed. The solution is: Do not bet the farm, bet the pig… This implies the importance of small-scale pilot projects in which the risk of failure is mitigated by the purposefully low exposure to the downside.

Do not bet the farm, bet the pig…

However, there is another risk at the organizational level. The risk of not finding individuals to run exploration projects! How "failure" in exploration projects is managed is critical – negative implications for the individuals involved will travel around the organization rapidly. A person who recommends "killing" an exploration project will be treated the same way as a person who proposes to kill exploitation, for instance the implementation of an IT project. Of course to recommend a "kill" in an exploitation project is not acceptable. However, in exploration projects the kill recommendation should be normal.

In organizations in which no differentiation is being made between exploitation projects and exploration projects, there is no understanding of the different levels of risk. Therefore, reprimanding leaders of exploration projects will substantially diminish the chances of other volunteers taking on the risk of exploration projects in the future.

The Ansoff-Matrix

Developed in the 1950s by Igor Ansoff, the Ansoff-Matrix (1957) is still a quite useful tool to assess the risk in innovation activities. The model is based on the two dimensions product (existing/new) and market (existing/new). In the quadrant of existing market/existing product it is clear that we are talking about continuous improvement. These are in ambidexterity terms the exploitation projects. In that quadrant the risk of failure is clearly the lowest.

At the other extreme, the quadrant of new market/new product, the risk is significantly higher. What is the link to ambidexterity? In this category we find the "exploration" projects. The risk is obviously highest in this new/new quadrant. What are the implications for exploration projects, which are often in exactly that quadrant? Indeed exploration projects carry the highest risks.

The innovator's dilemma

Over-engineering, well documented as the innovator's dilemma by Clayton Christensen (1997), is an additional source for risk, allowing new competitive space for possibly new competitors.

Christensen explains that even organizations which are seemingly doing the right things, such as engaging with lead users, can still fail. The logic is that by proactively co-developing with lead engineers at the customer base the resulting specifications may well overshoot even the demands of the most demanding customers. Christensen then explains the danger of overshooting in two or three subsequent product generations. The danger being that by focusing on the most demanding customers a gap is being created between the least demanding customers and the organization. These least demanding customers may just be overwhelmed by the technology available and may turn to an often new entrant who can offer a simple version, fulfilling basic requirements and at a competitive price.

How can organizations, whilst pushing for the next technical breakthrough, simultaneously find the right people and processes to create possibly new opportunities in less demanding applications?

Smartphone manufacturers immediately come to mind as example. In each new generation, for instance, there is better camera functionality. Now, originally advances from two-megapixels to say eight-megapixels really matter as the physical quality of the photo is significantly improved. At around the eight-mega-pixel level, however, the human eye is losing its ability to notice any significant improvement. Still, the engineers push further to 16 or even 32 mega-pixels. In times of aging populations you may wonder if this is not opening an opportunity for a low end producer whose mobile phone may only consist of two functions: to call and send text messages to the grandchildren... I am sure it is not going to be an easy task to persuade your top talents in engineering at one of the smart-phone manufacturers to take on that specific task.

However, the notion of over-engineering is not just confined to the engineering based industries. You can also see this quite vividly in the service industries. In fact, the most recent banking crises led to the admission of top bankers that the products developed ended up being too complex for both customers and bankers to understand. However, banks in the last few years have hired people with top degrees in mathematics, physics, and so on, in order to develop such differentiated products. Now, can you imagine that you today ask one of these highly educated people to develop an "index fund", a fund that is exactly mirroring the Dow-Jones or DAX Indices?

The risk of over-engineering is therefore twofold: First, it may lead to products and services that are too complicated for customers to understand and appreciate the extra value delivered. Secondly, over-engineering may open the door for low-cost competitors, offering simple, robust products and services. These low cost competitors then have a "foot in the door" in your market. They can then use the initial trust built with customers to move up the quality curve and may eventually compete also on the sophisticated, high quality end of the market.

Reducing Risk for Organization and Individuals

Case 1: Triple iii architecture

This case is taken from the manufacturing industry. Following a string of mergers and acquisitions, the organization had to consolidate. During this period of restructuring the process Triple iii (initiative, intrapreneurship, integration) was launched. At its launch it was designed to identify and develop talent in this newly merged organization.

It was designed through the initiative at head office with the support of key human resources (HR) stakeholders from the business units. In each cohort of participants some 20 individuals were identified through nominations via HR in the local business units (BUs).

Given the strategic context, the focus in this process was on the following:

Initiative: The pro-active identification of a business opportunity or the tackling of a concrete business re-engineering opportunity.

Intrapreneurship: The fostering of an entrepreneurial spirit inside the organization with a focus on change management.

Integration: At the time the strategic context inside the whole of the organization was on building an "integrated technology" organization. The Triple iii process therefore also had to address the opportunities for purposeful integration across business units.

The nomination process

Individual participants were identified through BU HR processes. However, once identified each individual had to demonstrate initiative:

- To suggest a concrete topic for an innovation/change project.
- To identify a sponsor, a senior executive whose role was to attest to the strategic significance of the project, to provide access to resources (budget, time, cross-functional), and to actively participate in the Triple iii process.
- To identify three to five supporters required to implement the initiative.

BOX 8.1 ILLUSTRATION

- Participant: Identified from department A.
- Project: To be identified by participant: for example, to re-engineer the interface between Departments A and B, Research and Development:

- Sponsor – senior executive who oversees both Departments A and B; the R&D Director;
- 3–5 supporters – individuals from both Departments A and B as key stakeholders.
- Task of the participant: To identify:
  - topic;
  - sponsor;
  - supporters.

The overall process

For each cohort of Triple iii participants, the overall process took approximately five months. The first two months consisted of pre-work – the identification of participants, topics, sponsor, and supporters. This was then followed by two workshops, three months apart. The purpose of the first workshop was to formally frame and launch the projects. During the three months between workshops, work on projects was completed on top of the normal workload. Then, workshop two entailed a review of the projects and a decision on how to proceed.

Engagement of the key stakeholders

In the pre-work phase the sponsor had to formally declare support of the project and agree with the project leader (participant) the expected outcomes and resources required, including inviting supporters. The three to five supporters had to be informed about the project, possibly being invited by the sponsor. Otherwise, their up-front involvement was limited.

The CEO had to invite participants and sponsors to the Triple iii process, being personally present at both the first and second workshops. Other management board members were available as discussants at fireside meetings and HR at BU level had to nominate participants and coach them during the process. This included checking on the stakeholder management (sponsor, supporters) at the local level. During the Triple iii workshops some HR experts acted as co-facilitators.

BOX 8.2 TRIPLE III OVERVIEW

Workshop 1

Day 1

Welcome and introduction from the HR director.

Expectations.

Roles: Internal/external.

Introduction to projects in four groups of five; forming of in-depth peer coaching environment. Experience so far with stakeholder management, expected challenges in the three-month project.

Plenum discussion: Patterns of projects. For instance, mix between change or innovation projects; internal vs external focus; patterns regarding experience with stakeholders; patterns regarding expected challenges.

Day 2:

Input: Managing change; change processes and the role of resistance.

Identifying and managing stakeholders; individual stakeholder map; peer coaching in terms of managing stakeholders.

Preparation of day 3: Project outline; flip charts; agenda; preparing the individual team space; topics to be discussed.

Day 3:

Auditorium offered large physical space. Twenty corners had been prepared by the participants as a precursor for working on the individual projects.

In the room initially 20 participants; later in the morning 80–100 supporters joined, who had been nominated in advance.

Welcome to supporters.

Work in individual group spaces.

Lunch.

Continue group work after lunch.

At around 3pm the CEO arrived and walked around to get an impression of the group before leading informal discussions.

Formal CEO address. This should cover the agenda for change, your contribution, importance of intrapreneurship: For example: "At the next meeting I expect to see results, progress; also, in times of change, we need to understand the patterns. What is propelling us forward, what is holding us back?" The role of middle managers in change and implementation should also be addressed.

Departure of supporters.

Informal discussion among participants continued. Spirits were very high...

Day 4 morning:

Debrief in peer groups. Turns taken to explain status of project. Participants were still on a high level of excitement. Then paradoxical intervention: How would you kill this project?

At first, a reaction of surprise. Then high energy in brainstorming:

Example: I would cancel meeting 1 day before, send number 2... Then solution mode: How do you handle these specific forms of resistance? This process in fact acted as an inoculation to combat resistance to be expected anyway. After this process the participants were ready for the real life challenges in their project work in the next three months.

Work in between modules:

Support from local HR/organizational development.

Some four weeks before the second workshop I received a string of calls from sponsors of the 20 projects launched that went mostly along the following lines:

Sponsor: "I got an invitation for your training program, I see that the CEO is coming, what is expected?"

Me: "Thank you very much for sponsoring this change project! At the next workshop we are reviewing progress made in specific change projects. We will identify patterns around what helps to accelerate change, what holds back."

Sponsor: "Aha, I understand."

You can imagine how the sponsor immediately called the project leader to inquire on the status of the project. This process led generally to a high level of engagement in the preparation for the second workshop.

Workshop 2

Day 1:

Peer group debriefing: Outcome of project work, the actual result. Debriefing on types of resistance experienced including the identification of patterns of resistance. Classroom discussion on forms of resistance experienced and strategies for dealing with specific forms of resistance.

Day 2:

Organizational culture.

Input on diagnosing organizational culture.

Insights from experiences made during project work.

Preparation of project market place, including the presentation of individual project content.

Insights on resistance and organizational culture.

Day 3 morning:

Location: Auditorium.

People present: 20 project leaders, 20 project sponsors plus the CEO.

Project market place.

Sponsors and CEO review individual projects.

Discussion of patterns of resistance, patterns of success factors, and the insights regarding organizational change culture.

Walk in the woods of participant and sponsor, to discuss informally project work and personal development opportunities.

Triple iii – the outcome

In summary, for each cohort of Triple iii:

- Work on 20 concrete projects.
- 20 participants/project owners.
- 80–100 supporters.
- 20 senior executives as project sponsors.
- CEO.

In two years in total 12 cohorts:

- Work on some 250 concrete projects.
- 250 participants/project owners.
- More than 1000 supporters.
- All senior executives as project sponsors.
- CEO.

Implications

Triple iii had started with a HR-logic, to develop the upcoming talent. However, after about three or four cohorts, the logic changed. It became apparent that the Triple iii approach addressed organizational development issues. The symptoms for these transitions are as follows:

- High success rate of projects, 67 per cent. Projects well documented and communicated.
- Coverage in corporate newspaper.
- Word of mouth – senior executives realized that within the Triple iii process corporate-wide visibility for their own area of responsibility could be

enhanced. In particular, the second workshop with the CEO and 20 senior executives in attendance was seen as opportunity for informal networking.
- Peer pressure for senior executives. As more and more senior executives had acted as sponsors it became apparent, that those who had not used the Triple iii platform started to pro-actively demonstrate engagement. Rather than nominating individuals for participation, senior executives put forward potential projects.

Insights from Case 1

With a focus on de-risking both at the organizational and individual level, the Triple-iii architecture offers the following insights:

- Project leader is protected by the sponsor and supported by up to five functional experts.
- Coalition: CEO, senior executives, and middle managers were united.
- Visibility: Activities took place openly, the rest of the organization could watch.
- Duration: The three-month timeframe provides challenge and focus.

Case 2: LEAD Architecture

This case example is based on Zurich Financial Services. The case is based on a joint presentation with Ian Owen at London Business School and the subsequent publication in the book *The Innovation Wave*.

> ### GOOD NEWS, BAD NEWS, 128 YEARS OF EXPERIENCE!
>
> In the first part I will give you a bit of background to our company and then explain the approach we at took to infuse innovation into what was a large, traditional organization. Ian will follow with a description of how he subsequently developed impressive innovation architecture at his regional level.

Zurich Financial Services is one of those large organizations that are good at what they do – we know what the rules of the game are, and we know the players in the industry. Until now, it had been about being smarter than the competition, and our key executives understood that competing was about using skill sets and capabilities such as target marketing better than the existing competitors. It was all about playing the existing game better.

The company has been around for 128 years and for more than 120 out of these 128 years we have been based on insurance. With its 68,000 employees, in 300 plus strategic business units in 65 odd countries, the company has traditionally been applying a highly decentralized operating model.

With such high levels of independence, the question often asked is not only 'How do we create shareholder value', but also, 'How can we take advantage of our presence in all those markets?' Of course, it is important to perform in all these markets. However, our shareholders expect that additional value be created from being part of a larger entity, Zurich Financial Services. This is why we needed more than just a leadership program. We needed an innovation architecture that would enable us to create an entity that provided greater value than the sum of its parts, leveraging our diversity and local market knowledge.

The need to change tack

In the past being better was sufficient to command a leading position in the industry. But new competitors are entering the market and things are changing. For example, in the United Kingdom, many 'non-finance' companies are entering the market such as grocery giant Tesco, clothing and food retailer Marks & Spencer, the multi-faceted Virgin, and Boots the Chemist, to name just a few. We felt that it was high time to respond and provide our key executives with tools to exercise 'Strategic Leadership', allowing the organization to make the shift from merely playing the game better, to proactively shaping the market of emerging financial services.

Traditionally, Zurich Financial Services would have tackled such a task locally. This time, following a sequence of mergers and acquisitions, the market expectation was to generate extra value from the corporate umbrella. Indeed, many advisors told us, 'Since you have spent so many years having a local focus, you should now turn your attention to the global needs of the organization'. However, we felt that too strong a swing from local to global focus would cause us to lose touch with local market needs. We wanted to do something very difficult instead, namely making sure that we keep the local touch whilst at the same time leveraging whatever possible at the global level.

A new course for the Zurich

To address the challenges we developed a four-step leadership process, LEAD (Leadership Education and Development). Each step involves workshops, lasting three to four days. The first workshop, which we call 'Activation', focuses on Value Creation and 'Strategies in converging markets' and on 'Innovation'. It is very much about creating a shared strategic agenda and to date 28 different groups and more than 700 executives have been through this process. But this was not enough. In fact, those who had attended the workshop wanted more than just a classroom exercise. They wanted to do it 'for real'.

In response, we created an innovation workshop with the sole purpose of generating new business concepts and new value creating processes. Over the last two years, the executives have generated 64 new business concepts/processes of which nine are already implemented. A further 15–20 per cent are currently in various stages of development. This is a remarkably high conversion rate.

The third workshop focuses on individual leadership development, providing the executive with an individual toolkit for achieving leadership results. The fourth workshop is focused on performance measurement at the organizational as well as individual level.

Charting unknown waters

The first two workshops provided had a measurable impact: when executives created winning ideas that added to the bottom line people began to listen. But how did we decide which business concepts to select? Let me briefly introduce the 'Innovation Landscape', a tool based on different categories of innovation – 10 different categories in our particular case. As well as expected categories such as 'product innovation' or 'core processes', this classification also included 'Business Model' innovation, which might for example, involve questioning how do we get paid? These categories provide a structure around which data can be added from an industry's history, to demonstrate where and when in the past innovations of a certain type had been introduced, creating a pattern – or landscape – that shows peaks and troughs of types of innovation at points in time.

We used the insights into the innovation landscapes for the Financial Services Industry in a number of ways. Clearly, we would not create most value if we focused on the same areas as everyone else. To give you an example from the computer industry: all players are competing on providing ever-higher performing PCs, showing as a peak in the 'performance' category on the computer industry innovation landscape. However, the 'distribution channels' category, at that point in time, would have shown as a trough. Gateway and Dell revolutionized the industry by focusing on the distribution channel, dealing direct with customers and thus changing the business model.

By creating and understanding the innovation landscape for the Financial Services Industry we were able to look at innovating in those areas where we would get the most 'bang for the buck;' i.e. where the effort would be most rewarded and where we could make a real difference. A very different approach to benchmarking, which essentially ensures that an organization is doing just the same as everyone else; just a bit better. Selecting ideas and concepts based on insights from an Innovation Landscape removes the randomness and creates the basis for innovation architecture, allowing us to innovate consecutively and at will.

Once we had identified the initiatives to be taken forward, the next step was to tailor the successful new concept to other markets – and remember we were operating in 60+ countries with the traditional view of 'my market is different'. Local protectionism was one of the reasons why the holistic approach we have taken – the common experience of more than 700 executives participating in the process, and easily understandable decision criteria – was so important. Through this approach we have achieved a level of involvement and buy-in for 'innovation' we would otherwise not have seen.

But even though, when looking at the concepts that were not taken forward we found that many great opportunities got sidelined because there was no 'natural' home for them. We therefore decided that initiatives launched at the corporate level needed to be supported by a 'local' innovation culture and supporting processes. And this is the point to hand over to my colleague Ian Owen who, having taken part in the corporate LEAD process, has taken the process into our UK operation.

The UK experience

I would like to start by emphasizing that the corporate center has been able to put together a remarkable program: the first module turned people who started the program by thinking "There's no need to innovate – you (from the center) just do not know how difficult it is", into a group sitting up saying, "My goodness! If we do not do something we are dead!"

The journey started in November 2000, with a senior management conference at a hotel near Heathrow for the UK's top 200 executives in the general insurance business. We collapsed the first two modules of the leadership program and innovation workshop. At the end of this some 40 ideas were generated – but generating the ideas was actually very, very easy. The big challenge was – how were we going to take them forward? I guess my appointment to spearhead the innovation projects was a first step – allocating responsibility. As I did not know much about innovation at the time, I felt reminded of the film 'A Field of Dreams' where they build a baseball pitch, hoping that people will come to play on it. And it has been a bit like that, people from different parts of the organization have offered to help and around this self-selected group we created something we called the Innovation Lab. So at this point in time we had established that innovation was crucial for us to succeed, and we had developed a number of ideas that people felt strongly about. People also started to feel safer about challenging the status quo, which was very important

However, what we needed to do was to create an environment where it felt safe to fail – not an easy task in an insurance company where people are highly risk averse and failure is generally followed by departure of the person responsible! What we wanted to create was not only an environment where people felt safe to fail; we actually wanted people to fail, as we could then learn from the mistakes. Another issue we were aware of is that you can keep generating ideas, and building on ideas, and developing the ideas – without ever achieving anything! So it was about having a passion for results from innovation and not just innovation for innovation's sake. In parallel we started developing processes that would support innovation – not formal manuals but guidelines so we could keep track of where we were. (See below)

Fairly arbitrarily we selected ten of the 40 ideas that had been generated in the senior management workshop. We then contacted the teams who had generated the ten ideas in order to select the five, which people felt the most passionate about. Once selected, each team was given up to £2,500 and four weeks to generate a detailed outline of their idea to present to the Innovation Panel. At this stage we were less concerned about the detailed finances than what the idea would mean for the organization and what would be required to take it to what we called 'proof of concept'. Zurich Financial Services was willing to invest a quarter of a million pounds on each idea to take it through to pilot stage. Interestingly, the vast majority has required far less funding than that.

Taking the ideas to proof of concept typically took around eight weeks. From there the team moved to a full-blown pilot and implementation.

In order to further foster and embed innovation into the company fabric, we developed a number of supporting concepts and processes, including:

- Rapid decision environment. We borrowed General Electric's Workout concept. Rather than relying on the senior people, often removed from the day-to-day business, to come up with suggestions about how to drive the organization forward you ask the people who are at the coalface. So frontline people would work together over a few days to generate solutions to a given operational or strategic problem. At the end of the few days they would come up with recommendations as to what needed to happen and how they would take it forward to implementation. The results were presented at what we call a town hall meeting with the sponsor (the person who set the problem in the first place) and relevant subject matter experts present. The purpose of the town hall meeting is to make a decision there and then. The rules of the game are that you cannot say, "We will think about it." You cannot just say, "No." If "no" is the answer, you have to state the reasons for the negative response. You can say "yes", or a "qualified yes", which normally means some additional work is required before a final decision can be made. So the point is to come to a go/no-go decision where people understand the reasoning behind the decision.

- Good Company. This concept involves taking a group of people out of the office environment for two or three days, to a hotel or similar venue where they are in an entirely different environment, that allows them to think outside the box, where they can work up ideas. The use of space, actors, props and sometimes customers is encouraged as this helps to generate and test the new ideas. Why actors? Actors are very good at creating different environments that people then walk into. The actors get our people to break out of their normal thinking patterns and do crazy things like speaking to mannequins as if they were customers. To give you another example, when people arrived to the last Good Company session yours truly was dressed up as a waiter serving the morning coffee. So people immediately got the message, that this was something different. At the end of the three-day session a group of senior people came in to be engaged in conversation around the ideas the group had generated. People learn from this that it is okay to do crazy things, that it is okay to take a risk, and that it is okay to fail as long as we learn.

The UK's experience also allowed us to tackle some of the innovations that really ought to have happened anyway. Breaking down the barriers to ownership and commitment helped us to bring in some very simple, yet effective innovations, including:

- A direct operation for small businesses. The UK has a very large commercial operation that deals with businesses both large and small. The main way of dealing with these customers is through insurance brokers. However, the Group does have a substantial direct business dealing directly with individual customers. So we decided to join the dots by taking the products from our commercial operation and joining them with the marketing and customer service expertise found in our direct operation, resulting in an ability to offer insurance directly to small businesses.

- Leveraging relationships with house builders. When you buy a new property, you will often get a National House Builder Certificate, which guarantees the build quality of the new house. Zurich offers something very similar; in fact, we are so strong in this market that the trade often calls the certificate "a Zurich." So we have a strong relationship with the building industry in the UK. But we were not exploiting this relationship by offering other financial services products related to house purchases such as home contents insurance or building insurance. How did we realize this? Simply because one person who had been frustrated about this missed opportunity that had not been realized over many, many years, gathered a team together, went to a Good Company event and took the idea all the way through to implementation.

Before summing up I would like to share a very interesting insight we gained from our program. We had three other ideas that have gone through this innovation process in the UK. When these groups came to present to the Innovation Panel they turned around to us and said, very passionately, 'We do not believe this is going to work for the following reasons'. So they were not turned down, but decided themselves that it would not work. That has then very been interesting for us as a group and has given us an opportunity to show that we were serious about celebrating failure. So we said, 'this is brilliant because you guys had the guts to say that you do not believe it will work after all. Now let us see what we can learn from that and how we can apply the insights to other projects we are doing.' Absolutely brilliant.

Where next?

Having had a number of the original ideas go through the system from concept to implementation we are now looking at how to generate more ideas. One way we are approaching this is by using our 'Young Tigers'. These are people who have been with the group not much longer than 18 months – the young, high flyers, the sort of person who is considered indispensable to the organization. We bring them together for a two-day workshop and ask them, if you were our competition, how would you beat Zurich? The ideas they come up with give us great inspiration on how and where to improve our services!

The innovation architecture we have put in place across the organization will also allow us to start using groups across our business units to address certain customer segments on a global scale. We do support regional developments but are keen to leverage benefits and programs that reach across the entire group. Our industry is converging, changing and morphing all the time, whether we like it or not. The question is, are we being merged, morphed and converged or are we actually actively shaping and leading the changes? And our intention is very clearly to actively shape our future.

Critical success factors

We believe that the Zurich Financial Services experience of innovation has yielded some important insights for other organizations wishing to shake up their traditional business model.

1) Understand the terrain in which you are operating.

2) Look for external funding. External scrutiny helps to cut through the internal politics as many opportunities get killed because there is no natural home for them. If you've got outside investors they force the issue and they increase the urgency of delivery because they want to get out of the business at some point and see a return on their investment.

3) Incentivize the innovators.

4) Make decisions as rapidly as possible and don't look for excuses why something can't be done. Explore the orthodoxies in your industry and look at ways to change them.

5) Create architecture around innovation so that you can actually innovate consecutively and not randomly.

6) Celebrate and learn from failures.

Jens Maier and Ian Owen, Zurich Financial Services:

> Bettina von Stamm (2003) "Finding the fish and aligning the fleet – Making Innovation an every day capability" in *The Innovation Wave*: reproduced with permission.

Insights from Case 2

With a focus on de-risking both at the organizational and individual level, the LEAD architecture offers the following insights:

- Top-down corporate initiative providing a platform for concrete corporate innovation projects.
- Local architectures: Experience at corporate level led to the purposeful creation of organizational capabilities at the local level.
- Risk: Provide a platform for experiencing risk and failure.

Case 3: Innovate! Architecture

In an IT organization the CEO had worked with the innovation landscape concept and realized that in his organization and his business the focus for innovation was almost solely on technology, better products. Subsequently, the CEO started an innovation initiative starting with his top management team.

In the half-day workshop (Workshop 1) the innovation agenda over and beyond product innovation was agreed, as well as a process for exploration projects that was communicated in a global video conference call to the global top 50 executives. Remarkable in this process was the collective realization that:

- The top management team had to be united behind the exploration process.
- Individuals of the top team had to act as sponsors for concrete exploration projects.

- Orthodoxies were purposefully identified: As a potential hindrance of innovation beyond products as well as a source for idea generation, by purposefully turning the orthodoxies on their heads.

The top 50 executives were invited to nominate topics and potential project leaders to purposefully address the types of innovation underutilized. Four weeks later ten project leaders armed with their initial project topics came together for a two-day workshop. In a brief welcome the CEO stressed the importance for exploration and explained both the strategic context and the concrete exploration process. In particular the expectation was communicated that in the three-month long exploration phase a "prototype" was to be developed and a recommendation for either accelerate or kill.

On day one the initial ten projects went through a structured process, consisting of conceptual frameworks as well as elements of peer coaching. On day two the project ideas were shaped further to include identification and management of stakeholders; the necessary resources for a three-month exploration phase were also identified. The day was concluded with individual presentations to the project sponsor. The outcome was that ten projects and ten project leaders had a clear project plan for the following three months. In the following three months the project leaders were coached by their sponsor and by the process facilitator.

Workshop review

After three months a two-day review workshop took place for the ten projects and project leaders. Day one focused on the project leaders, in order to allow them to hone the recommendation they were planning to give to the sponsors on day two.

The challenge for the project managers was to commit to a clear recommendation to either accelerate or kill. At the beginning of day one the majority of the project leaders were unsure. They claimed that yes three months was too short a time, they wanted to test a few more ideas and to collect additional data. However, through a structured process consisting of coaching and peer coaching each project leader had, at the end of day one, a clear recommendation as well as a collection of insights about the concrete exploration process, including resistance and orthodoxies encountered.

On Day two was the presentation to the sponsors. The whole management team had individually at least been in the role of sponsor to one of the projects. Under external facilitation the management team had a clear process in place:

- Clear criteria (strategic/financial) for accelerate or kill.
- 10 minute presentation by project leader.
- Questions and answers.
- Decision making by management team; with the project leader present in the room during that decision-making process.

The results were as follows: Seven projects accelerated, three projects killed. The interesting process observation was that the highest scrutiny by the management team was given to projects with a kill recommendation. Here, the project leaders were in particular challenged as to whether they had used the appropriate level of resources, time in particular. The management team wanted to understand whether the project leaders were looking to take the easy way out.

The management team was very attentive to the way the decisions were communicated to the rest of the organization. It was the first time that the organization had addressed explicitly the notion of exploration projects. Therefore, how does the management team deal with failure, with project leaders who recommend killing a project? Care was taken that project leaders were equally rewarded for recommending to accelerate or to kill a project.

As the CEO said in the meeting to the management team: If we are seen punishing project leaders coming back with a kill recommendation, how can we find new project leaders for the next wave of exploration projects? However, what we should be clear about is that we do not tolerate inaction.

Insights from Case 3

With a focus on de-risking both at the organizational and individual level, the innovate architecture offers the following insights:

- Top-down initiative, engaging the entire top team.
- Top team as sponsors: All members of the top team engaged in their role as sponsors.
- Orthodoxies: Clarity on orthodoxies as source for resistance and source for idea generation.
- Review: Transparent review process in terms of accelerating or "killing" of projects and rewarding action takers, regardless of outcome.

The Roles in Leading Ambidexterity

This book has emphasized throughout the fact that individuals can be in the possible roles of:

- Architects.
- Project leaders.
- Recipients.

What are the implications of de-risking ambidexterity? Let us start with the role of the architect.

Architect

In the role of the architect, the task is to monitor the environment and to determine the level of change/innovation required. Based on these insights it is then critical to create a sense of urgency so that an unfreezing inside the organization can take place. Any new change initiative in an organization will be greeted with the "why?" question. The architect should have a compelling answer to that question!

In numerous workshops with corporate clients literally hundreds of change/innovation projects have been reviewed. Using the Kotter model already introduced in Chapter 2 as a guide, the picture is very usually very clear when you plot the patterns of successful and unsuccessful projects on the same chart. Successful projects almost always score very highly on the first three stages of the Kotter model, creating a sense of urgency, building a strong leadership coalition, and creating a compelling vision. In unsuccessful projects the reverse is true, very low scores on these first three stages in the Kotter model. What is this telling us? It means the "architect" has failed! The best project manager cannot rescue a project if the architect has not fulfilled his/her role.

Failing at the first three stages of the Kotter model implies that the architect has not developed a sufficient answer to the "why?" question. This summarizes the biggest risk in the role of an architect.

BOX 8.3 THE KOTTER MODEL

1) Create a sense of urgency.

2) Establish strong leadership coalitions.

3) Create a compelling vision.

4) Communicate the vision for the change.

5) Empowering others with comprehensive options to act.

6) Generate short-term and visible successes.

7) Consolidate gains and successes.

8) Institutionalize new measures in the everyday routine.

Now, the risks described above only set in once the architect has already started an initiative. Therefore, we should also pay attention to the much larger risk: Doing nothing! If there are significant changes in the environment and the architect decides to ignore these changes and still focus on exploiting the established business instead of also using exploration, the risk is that their days in the role of architect are numbered! Beware the one-handed manager!

Beware the one-handed manager!

So, how can the architect then de-risk the role for both the individual and the organization?

- Identify senior executives, members of the top team, to be in the role of sponsor.
- Identify a number of individuals who are qualified to be project leaders.
- Install a robust process for ambidexterity, with clear roles and responsibilities.

Sponsor

The role of the sponsor is to provide the hierarchical go-ahead for a project to be started. This go-ahead should be based upon:

- Permission to explore an opportunity in the pre-defined space.
- Clear outcome expectations to explicitly include accelerate or kill options.
- Access to supporters from across the organization.
- Provision of (small) budget regarding time and money.

Project leader

The architect has identified an individual to drive the project. This is obviously done in alignment with the project sponsor (more often than not, the architect also acts as project sponsor…).

Now the implementer has to really move into the project mindset. This means the individual has to win the hearts and minds of key stakeholders. As the project leader the individual has to address all the local resistance issues.

Summary

Exploration projects are more risky than exploitation projects. Therefore, the focus in this chapter was on the nature of de-risking for both the individual and the organization.

The Ansoff-Matrix, even so many years after its invention, is still a good starting point. Obviously, the level of risk to both individual and organization is quite different when you innovate in the space of existing markets/existing products compared to in the space of a new market and new products. The first challenge is very much around exploitation. The individuals running innovation projects in this space can get a lot done in their role as manager. Now, in the new/new space the role of the manager will not be sufficient. Here, the role of a leader is required, to challenge the status quo, to explore and shape the future.

Clayton Christensen more recently pointed out the innovator's dilemma in that, by focusing on the high-end customers, after a few iterations a gap at the bottom end of the market may appear. This gap may then attract new competitors who may enter with no-frills solutions. This new entry may then get a foothold in the market from which to also attack the profitable parts of the incumbent. This is the risk of over-engineering. This risk is primarily apparent in high tech businesses but also in specialist based services such as banking or accountancy.

Using the Triple iii case example, the chapter then focused on the risk for different roles as architect, project leader, and implementer. Although, in terms of risk, the focus was very much on the individual in that role. However, individual failures in these roles have also a big impact on the overall organization both in terms of performance and impact on the culture of innovation in the organization.

De-risking exploration projects: core elements

As we have seen, to take on exploration projects is risky for both individuals as well as the organization. So here are the core elements to watch out for:

Architecture:

- Clear agenda of which types of innovation should be addressed in exploration projects.
- Defined start and clear review deadline within a tight time frame of, for example, three months.

- Expectation to create a prototype, the look and feel that can be evaluated.
- Clear expectation of a recommendation of either to kill or to accelerate.
- Senior executive to be in role of sponsor to give permission, access to resources, cross-functional experts – the supporters.
- Identification of cross-functional experts as part of the project team.
- Process: Not to ask for ROI at the initiation of the project, ROI has to be addressed at the review workshop.
- Review: Clear decision on to either kill or to accelerate. Avoid project clutter or worse create undead projects.
- Reward for clear recommendation to kill/accelerate independent of outcome. Punish inaction in exploration phase.

The senior executive in the role of sponsor has to be very clear about the difference between sponsoring exploitation versus an exploration project. Senior executives who are used to sponsoring exploitation projects will have a tool set they have tested well during their careers consisting, among other things, of:

- ROI; each project should at initiation meet a hurdle rate expectation of say 12 per cent ROI.
- Failure; an unsuccessful exploitation project leads to the punishment of the project leader. For instance failure to implement an IT project.
- Project duration; depending on the industry, senior executives have experience with exploitation projects lasting many months, even years.

In exploration projects all three experiences need to be challenged:

- ROI; at initiation it is almost impossible to come up with an ROI figure. In fact part of the exploration project is to determine whether a robust ROI figure can be determined as a basis for deciding whether to accelerate or kill the project.
- Failure; the recommendation to kill an exploration project is not "failure." It is just a valid outcome of the exploration phase. Indeed, failing

fast may save the organization lots of resources that would otherwise be wasted.

- Project duration; Exploration projects should be short. In about three months it is usually possible to create a "prototype" for innovating beyond product performance.

The project leader should not start an exploration project without the explicit support from a senior executive in the role as sponsor. The support of the sponsor is critical in terms of:

- Managing expectations; prototype; kill/accelerate.
- Resources such as time and budgets on top.
- Access to cross-functional experts inside the organization.

Summary: Part II

In the second part of this book it is attempted to offer possible solutions to the challenges around building ambidextrous organizations and developing ambidextrous leaders.

1) Bandwidth

   Ambidexterity calls for both individuals and organizations to use both hands. The fact that both individuals and organizations usually have a dominant hand was addressed. At the beginning of Part II the concept of "bandwidth" was defined. The bandwidth describes the capacity at both individual and organizational level to use both hands. The recommendation is to develop bandwidth at both the individual and the organizational level.

2) Ambidexterity as organizational capability: Linking individual development and organizational development

   The opportunity in linking both key processes to develop ambidextrous leaders and to build ambidextrous organizations. Leveraging work on exploration projects, to linking to individual development programs. Anchor new capability as a platform from which to launch innovation at will.

3) Role of end customer – The segment of one

The Nespresso model: Many business-to-business (B2B) industries envy Nespresso for having implemented the concept to directly building a meaningful relationship with the ultimate customers. Numerous efforts in exploration activities across industries are targeted at building that type of relationship. This is not new, as many of us remember the "Intel inside" campaign from the early 1990s. Today, talk about personalized medicine is not only supported by better IT and social networks, but also through the ultimate individualization tool, the availability of DNA analyses at very low cost.

4) Scouting – purposefully looking beyond

The role of big data and the role of small data. The importance of the role of ethnography as an approach to observe the context of customers and to deduct implications for new products and services.

5) Collaboration

Building the ambidextrous organization implies to purposefully build the capability of "collaboration" inside an organization. Exploration means that a number of internal departments and functions need to be collaborating. This goes above and beyond the usual suspects of R&D and marketing and sales. The model of the ten types of innovation includes a few other departments such as finance (revenue model) and legal (networking arrangements). This is just the internal view. As organizations engage in shaping game innovation they immediately have to partner with organizations from different industries. This necessity is pushing up the importance of "collaboration" as a key organizational capability.

6) The role of failure

Exploration implies experimentation, implies the likelihood of failure. Most organizations are, rightly so, intolerant of failure. However, that reference point is based on normal operations, where of course we want to see a zero-defect culture. In terms of project work the reference is based on exploitation projects. Again, here is the expectation that the exploitation project is being completed on time and on budget. An ambidextrous organization is intolerant of failure in exploitation and embraces the notion of "failing fast" as a core element of exploration.

7) The role of leaders – de-risking

In building an ambidextrous organization your leadership role is critical. As architect, you need to ensure that both exploitation and exploration can co-exist. In particular in exploration, with its high risk of "failure," both the individual project leader and the organization need to be protected. This can be achieved through a purposeful structure of sponsorship, allocation of know-how over and beyond R&D and a well-structured review process. In your role as leader it is your task to build ambidexterity as an organizational capability.

Conclusion

Ambidexterity is not an Option

Megatrends such as aging population, mobility, and green energy are creating new opportunities. The question is who can capture the value of these opportunities? Is it the start-up companies? Is it the ubiquitous Google, Apple, or Facebook? What about the existing organizations in industries such as pharmaceuticals, energy, insurance, telecoms, and so on? Can they take advantage of the opportunities presented? Moreover, what is the risk to their core business today, will they lose their relevance as much as the manufacturers of typewriters did many years ago?

These established organizations have to be able to use both hands simultaneously to conduct both exploitation and exploration: making next quarter's performance numbers in the existing business, whilst at the same time exploring these new opportunities.

Ambidexterity is not an option. The only question is: Do you address it proactively or defensively? Proactively implies that you set in motion a deliberate process to exploit the existing business whilst simultaneously exploring new business opportunities beyond the existing business. Defensively means that a wholly new intruder may shape the next phase of your industry, as happened to Blackberry and Nokia when Apple created, with the iPhone, a whole new category – the smartphone market.

Building Ambidextrous Organizations – the Key Challenges

Convergence between markets and technologies happens all around us. Leaders have to steer their organizations through this unchartered territory. Traditional management approaches will not work: Both leaders and their organizations have to be geared towards ambidexterity. This means with one hand exploiting the current business and with the other exploring new opportunities provided through converging technologies and markets. This has got implications at two levels:

1) The organization: How can the whole organization embrace the simultaneous processes of exploitation and exploration?
2) The individual leader: How can you personally balance the different demands of both exploiting and exploring?

Organizational challenges

Ambidexterity (improving today's business and experimenting with opportunities beyond the current business) requires an awareness to put it on the strategic agenda, the creation of robust processes for exploration (on top of the normally well-functioning exploitation processes), the ability to deal with failure, to move from prediction/forecasting to having a point of view, the ability to win partners (even from other industries), and to influence that partnership.

Individual challenges

The challenges depend on which role you are taking. As *architect* you have to put the topic on the strategic agenda and help build robust processes around exploration. As *project leader* for an exploration project you have to de-risk the project for yourself as much as for the organization. You have to demand the appropriate infrastructure – process, resources, and scorecard for success from your sponsor. As *implementer*, you will have to take a successful "prototype" and make it stick in the organization and scale it up fast. Being able to deal with resistance will be a key factor for success.

Prerequisites for Success

On balance, you need the capability to do convergence engineering at both the organizational and individual level. At the organizational level to acknowledge that you have to create a point of view and to win over important partners with key capabilities required. At the individual level, you require the ability to deal with ambiguity. This means being able to influence (oftentimes without "power") other people and organizational partners.

Why is This Important for You and for Your Organization?

The reward is high: Some 20 years of academic research have demonstrated that ambidextrous organizations outperform their rivals.

Individuals who can demonstrate their own competence in applying ambidexterity, in whatever role, will be in very high demand in the coming years. Your courage and your role modeling, however, will have a tremendous impact beyond any specific project experiences. Your personal story of having avoided the trap of the one-handed manager and embracing the role of the ambidextrous leader can set the example that can energize your organization to grab the opportunities presented – and avoid the trap for your organization of going down the route of the typewriter business.

Leadership challenges

This book, throughout, addresses the importance of individuals shaping an organization. The concept of the two roles for individuals as managers and leaders is paramount. The leadership research demonstrates that leadership at all levels is the hallmark of successful organizations. The concept of leader/manager implies that it is not dependent on hierarchy but that it is driven by two different roles an individual can take in an executive function. In the context of ambidexterity, the notion of "exploitation" is very much associated with an individual taking on the role as a manager. Exploration explicitly calls for individuals to accept their role as leader.

Ambidexterity challenges you in your role as both manager and leader. In normal exploitation mode, you are challenged in your role as manager. This means you have to "do things right" to implement according to agreed deadlines and budgets. However, in "exploration" projects, you are expected to challenge the status-quo, to identify in order to "do the right things." This is accepting and fulfilling your role as a "leader." Your personal leadership challenge consists in being ambidextrous: With one hand focusing on exploitation – very much akin to your role as manager – and the other hand focusing on exploration – just like your role as leader.

Why does this matter? Organizations that have ambidextrous leaders seem to outperform those organizations that have to rely on a structural solution in which one-handed managers either focus on exploitation or in a separate unit focus on exploration.

What are the individual leadership challenges beyond the ability to use both hands?

Influencing (without power): The personal competence to influence partners from different functions, organizations or even from different industries and align around a common goal.

Intrapreneurship: The ability and willingness to drive innovation and change from within the organization. This is different from entrepreneurship in which individuals are driven to create their own story, in their own organization. Intrapreneurs thrive on the power of an existing organization, its reputation, and global presence as a precursor for having a seat at the table when convergence is driving changes in global markets.

Processes for Exploration

The challenge for both organizations and their leaders is to distinguish between exploitation and exploration processes. In this book, a case has been made for treating exploration projects differently and not applying the innovation funnel at the start of an exploration project. By their very nature exploration projects are set up to innovate "beyond" – also beyond the "strategic fit" as manifested in the organization's previous year's strategic plan.

The case is made for the fact that exploration projects should be run through a different process:

- Initial short duration (approximately three months).
- Project leader and supporters engaged on a part-time basis, on-top of their normal commitments.
- Clear expectation at the beginning to develop a "kill" or "accelerate" recommendation based on the business case for a prototype.

Secondly, to start an exploration project with the request for a return-on-invest (ROI) statement is not logical and can even be wrong. This is obviously in stark contrast to the usual practice in exploitation projects. However, at the start of an exploration project the data is simply not there.

This approach is not suggested to replace the normally well-functioning funnel approach for exploitation projects. Indeed, the exploration project can be viewed as a pre-phase to the funnel concept. In case of a recommendation to accelerate the project, at that stage it can then enter the funnel process with its normal stage-gating milestone steps.

Mindset Challenges

Ambidextrous organizations are not start-up organizations. Ambidextrous organizations have a history, a track record. Going forward it seems to be prudent to explicitly pay attention to the shared mindset developed and to honor the past successes. In successful organizations and industries it is very common that strong dominant mindsets emerge. The question is when do these dominant mindsets become blinkers?

Orthodoxies

In normal business situations orthodoxies are always present. However, nobody ever talks about them. Moreover, the orthodoxies are not only present, but the core orthodoxies transcend organizations in the same industry.

What are the consequences? Orthodoxies are like a magnet to pull the organization back to its core. From an ambidexterity perspective, orthodoxies pull organizations to innovate in exploitation mode. However, they will work like antibodies to fight exploration projects. Orthodoxies as a source for idea generation may sound contradictory at first, as exploration projects will be fought by the orthodoxies. That may be the case, but when you take an orthodoxy and turn it on its head, then a whole new set of ideas will emerge.

Solution: Linking Individual and Corporate Development

In building ambidextrous organizations we need ambidextrous leaders.

Increasing the bandwidth of both the individual and the organization is the key challenge regarding ambidexterity. In Chapter 5 the role of a "corporate university" (CU) in building the bandwidth at both the individual and the organizational level was discussed. This is, of course, an extreme form of "leadership development," which is most likely to be applied by large organizations. Although, over the years, we have also witnessed many smaller organizations moving this way as well.

Why focus on CUs instead of just leadership development? The term "university" is critical to our debate on ambidexterity because universities are equally engaged in two core activities: Teaching and research. In terms of a "corporate" university you can see immediately the link:

Exploitation – Teaching

Exploration – Research

Therefore, by definition a "corporate university" can provide the glue between the individual development process and the corporate development process by simultaneously linking exploitation ("teaching") to exploration ("researching").

Solution Scouting

How can we best scout the unknown territory for exploration success?

In exploration, by definition, we cannot rely on predicting and forecasting. How can we establish the necessary data for shaping game strategies, for putting a stake in the ground?

Some organizations use technology scouting, often guided by the Gartner Hype Cycle, to keep focused on how new technologies can offer new opportunities. Scouting picks up technological developments and can build early relationships with start-ups in order to master these technological advances quickly.

New technology platforms make it feasible to establish the direct link with the end-user. The opportunity is often described as "Can we not be the Nespresso in our industry?" or "what is our equivalent to Intel inside?" Therefore, in order to address the appropriate solutions companies in a B2B2C setting, increasingly for exploration projects, go beyond the normal B-customer and embrace the opportunities around the end-user. Scouting will then have to include purposefully understanding this end-user and cutting out the middleman, often completely new territory for the organization.

So how can we then understand the end-user? By applying "big data" perhaps? It is difficult to assimilate and understand the plethora of data from various sources. It was for this reason that the Gartner Group moved the topic of big data in August 2014 to the category of "disillusionment."

However, it would be wrong to pre-maturely write off big data as a source for looking beyond. It may take a bit of time to identify smart ways of dealing with issues of data connectivity, public acceptance, regulatory approval, and also developing some smart predictive modeling tools. It may be possible to apply big data approaches to address problems such as Alzheimer's disease. In that case the individual, the health insurers and societies determined by aging populations would benefit. It is unlikely that so many potential benefits will not trigger smart solutions; hence, big data will remain a dominant source for scouting, whatever it may be called.

Looking at the role of anthropology and its specific form, ethnography, can help organizations to understand the end-user better through small data, rather than big data. More companies are using advanced technology and ethnographers to document people's behaviors and analyze the choice patterns of those individuals.

Identifying individual end-users is critical because insights generated by understanding a few customers in depth, in their individual context, can generate a platform for testing new, customer-centric approaches which could be very beneficial to the end-user.

Solution: Convergence Engineering

Collaboration is the key to taking advantage of convergence. Collaboration across organizational functions, but also across organizations and even industries, is essential in order to assemble the required capabilities. Just because convergence takes place around us does not mean that we can play an active role. It requires purposeful engineering.

Private Equity partnerships provide us with helpful models on how to manifest these collaborative partnerships in exploration activities, in collaboration trust, and firm agreements on roles and responsibilities matter.

The role of eco-systems: To think about collaboration in terms of eco-systems, spanning not only industries but also geographies. This provides the basis for building a new organizational capability: eco-system mapping. This will allow the organization to purposefully take advantage of local and global eco-systems for collaboration.

The role of a vision in convergence engineering: As we are in unchartered waters the common vision of the partners is even more important. This vision acts as the lighthouse to keep the exploration project on track. Corporate venturing: Initially started inside large organizations to foster exploration projects within the industry, these corporate venturing units are also increasingly used to foster cross-industry collaboration. These corporate venturing units have the potential to become the engineers facilitating local and global eco-systems.

The role of customer-centric solutions: Ubiquitous technology (mobile, cloud, Internet of everything, social media) has created the perfect storm. The global winner is the individual! This segment of one will demand and will receive customer-centric solutions, effectively becoming the key driver for converegence.

De-risking: The role of leaders. In your role as architect you have to ensure that both exploitation and exploration can co-exist. Exploration, the more risky form of innovation, needs to be protected. The higher risks involved have to be mitigated at both the organizational and the individual level. Playing a critical role is the notion of "failure." As an architect it is your role to protect the individuals and the organization. However, it is also your task to avoid the stigma of "failure" in exploration projects.

The role of failure: Exploration implies experimentation, and therefore implies the likelihood of failure. Most organizations are, rightly so, intolerant of failure. However, that reference point is based on normal operations, where of course we want to see a zero-defect culture. In terms of project work the reference is based on exploitation projects. Again, here is the expectation that the exploitation project is being completed on time

An ambidextrous organization is intolerant of failure in exploitation and embraces the notion of "failing fast" as a core element of exploration

and on budget. An ambidextrous organization is intolerant of failure in exploitation and embraces the notion of "failing fast" as a core element of exploration.

For both Nokia and Blackberry it did not take long to fall off the cliff. One day you are one of the most admired companies the next day you look at the abyss of being irrelevant. Yes, you may have the highest market share and you have done really well to defend that position with a presumably loyal customer base and a very competitive cost position. The newspapers and the business writers may praise you for your achievements.

By focusing on existing markets you may not pay enough attention so that around you new markets are being shaped, oftentimes by players you would never have considered serious competitors in your "core" market. Even a high tech veteran like Intel who had weathered the storms of many technical revolutions had to shape up to fully address the shift from desktop/laptop devices to truly mobile devices such as smartphones or ipads/tablet computers for which all of a sudden other competitors had the better chips.

Most innovation projects fail. Now that includes exploitation and exploration projects. In terms of ambidexterity we should look at failure differently. Yes, an exploitation project such as introducing a new IT system can fail. However, given the nature of the task and the fact that so many organizations have successfully done it will reflect – rightly so – on the project leader. Therefore, after failing in that project the project leader should be severely questioned why the expectations were not met. Now, that is different in an exploration project. Here it is like sending out four ships from an island to explore whether there are any other islands to the north, south, east or west.

Now, here the scorecard is different. Yes, everyone will celebrate the hero who has discovered the adjacent island in the north. But do you punish the ones who did not find other islands in the south, west and east? Of course not! In fact you have to praise the project leaders for having taken the personal risk of exploration. The fact that they could not find another island in these three directions has helped everyone on the island to understand their environment better. "Punishment" for the leaders of exploration projects should be reserved for the situation that they have not tried hard enough.

Organizations especially with an "outperformance culture" or a "zero defect culture" are challenged to acknowledge that a different approach to "failure" is required between exploration and exploitation projects. In organizational cultures like the ones described above, the architects of ambidexterity are really challenged to explain the rules and scorecards for exploration. However, everyone in the organization will watch very carefully what happens to project leaders whose exploration projects fail. If the impression is that these individuals are being punished, it is going to be almost impossible to identify competent project leaders for the next exploration projects. For the organization as a whole this process can turn out to be disastrous. It can lead to the organization staying focused on the existing business and over time may even become irrelevant like the typewriter manufacturers.

The role of processes: The innovation funnel process is being used successfully in exploitation projects. However, to use the same process for exploration projects is counterproductive.

Exploration processes should lead to the developement of a "prototype" and an associated rough business plan in a short period, say three months. This should provide the basis for making a decision to either kill or to accelerate. Especially in the case of a decision to "kill" an exploration project, the project leader and the team will not have lost face. This is just normal business practice, implementing the "failing fast" principle.

Summary

This book has identified some of the key drivers for convergence between industries. This convergence will challenge organizations to proactively shape new markets and/or avoid being "disrupted" in core markets.

Organizations will have at least to respond to these challenges. However, many organizations will look at these developments as a major opportunity – how can we take advantage? Now? Likewise, those organizations retrenching, playing it (presumably) safe will have to stay extremely vigilant: Both Blackberry and Nokia provide examples of how close the line is between admiration and obsolescence…

Customers in many industries expect organizations to be customer centric. Despite a lot of lip-service most organizations still have a huge challenge ahead of themselves to deliver against the expectations of their ever demanding customers.

The ambidextrous organization can provide the expected customer centricity by exploring the new while exploiting the now.

Beware the one-handed manager, welcome the ambidextrous leader!

References

Allport, G. W., & Odbert, H. S. (1936), Trait names: A psycholexical study. *Psychological Monographs*, 47: 211.

Ansoff, I. (1957) Strategies for diversification, *Harvard Business Review*, 35(5): 113–24.

Bruch H., & Bieri S. (2003) Hilti 2003. Maintaining a proactive sense of urgency. University St. Gallen case study.

Bruch, H. & Ghoshal, S. (2002) Beware the busy manager. *Harvard Business Review*, February.

Carr, N. G. (1999) Visualizing innovation. *Harvard Business Review*, September–October: 16.

Christensen, C. (1997) *The Innovator's Dilemma*. Boston: Harvard Business School Press.

Cooper, R. (1990) Stage-gate systems: A new tool for managing new products. *Business Horizons*, 33(3): 44–55.

Costa, P. T., Jr. & McCrae, R. R. (1992) *Revised NEO Personality Inventory (NEO-PI-R) and NEO Five-Factor Inventory (NEO-FFI) Manual*. Odessa, FL: Psychological Assessment Resources.

Crama, P., de Reyck, P., Degraeve, Z., & Chong W. (2007) Research and development project valuation and licensing negotiations at Phytopharm plc. *Interfaces*, 37(5): 472–87.

Duncan, R. (1976) The Ambidextrous Organization: Designing Dual Structures for Innovation. In R. H. Kilman, L. R. Pondy, & D. Stevens (eds) *The Management of Organization Design, Vol 1*. New York: North Holland, pp 167–88.

Dutcher J. (2014) What is big data? Datascience@berkeley; September 3.

Financial Times (2014) World will have 13 super-aged nations by 2020. August 6.

Gibson, C. B., & Birkinshaw, J. (2004) The antecedents, consequences and mediating role of organizational ambidexterity. *Academy of Management Journal*, 47: 209–26.

Hewitt, G. (2013) Creating value in the new business landscape. Unpublished working paper.

Keeley, L., Pikkel, R., Quinn, B., & Walters, H. (2013) *Ten Types of Innovation*. Hoboken: John Wiley & Sons.

Kelley, T. and Kelley, D. (2013) *Creative Confidence*. London: Crown Business.

Kotter, J. P. (1996) *Leading Change*. Boston: Harvard Business School Press.

Leslie, J. B, & Van Velsor, E. (1996) *A Look at Derailment Today*. Brussels: Center for Creative Leadership.

Levinthal, D., & March, J. G. (1993) The myopia of learning. *Strategic Management Journal*, 14: 95–112.

March, J. G. (1991) Exploration and exploitation in organizational learning. *Organization Science*, 2: 71–87.

Markides, C. C., & Geroski, P. A. (2004) *Fast Second*. San Francisco: Jossey-Bass.

Mason, H. (2011) Riding the fifth wave. *Global Corporate Venturing*, February: 21–3.

Mathonet, P. Y., & Meyer, T. (2008) *J-Curve Exposure: Managing a Portfolio of Venture Capital and Private Equity*. Chichester: John Wiley & Sons.

McKinsey Quarterly (2014) What strategists need: a meeting of the minds. *McKinsey Quarterly* number 3, 38–51.

Meyer, T., & Mathonet, P. Y. (2011) *Beyond the J-Curve*. Chichester: John Wiley & Sons.

Meyer, T. (2014) *Private Equity Unchained*. Basingstoke: Palgrave Macmillan.

Prahalad, C. K., & Hamel, G. (1990) The core competence of the corporation. *Harvard Business Review*, May–June: 79–91.

Prahalad, C. K (2010) Why is it so hard to do the obvious? *Harvard Business Review*, June: 36.

Prahalad, C. K., & Bettis, R. A. (1986) The dominant logic: New linkage between diversity and performance. *Strategic Management Journal*, 7: 485–501.

Press, G. (2014) Forbes, 12 big data definitions: what's yours? *Forbes*, September 3.

Raisch, S., & Birkinshaw, J. (2008) Organizational ambidexterity: Antecedents, outcomes, and moderators. *Journal of Management*, 34, 375–409.

Salvador, T. et al (2013) *Radical Flux*. Intel Books (digital edition).

Sattelberger, T. (2014) Rethinking corporate universities. *World Commerce Review*, March.

Senge, P. (1990) *The Fifth Discipline: The Art and Practice of the Learning Organization*. New York: Doubleday.

Singer N. (2014) Intel's sharp eyed social scientist. *New York Times*, February 15.

Simsek, Z. (2009) A typology for aligning organizational ambidexterity's conceptualizations, antecedents and outcomes. *Journal of Management Studies*, 46: 864–94.

Tuckman, B. W. (1965) Developmental sequence in small groups. *Psychological Bulletin*, 63(6): 384–99.

Tushman, M. L., & O'Reilly, C. A. (1996) Ambidextrous organizations: Managing evolutionary and revolutionary change. *California Management Review*, 38: 8–30.

Ulrich D. (1997) Measuring human resources: An overview of practice and a prescription for results. *Human Resource Management*, 36(3): 303–20.

Von Stamm, B. (2003) *The Innovation Wave*. Chichester: John Wiley & Sons.

Wheatley, M. (2014) *Gartner's Hype Cycle: Big Data's on the Slippery Slope*. Gartner, August 18.

Further Reading

Bennis, W. (1989) *Why Leaders can't Lead*. San Francisco: Jossey-Bass.

Bruch H., & Ghoshal S. (2003) Unleashing organizational energy. *Sloan Management Review*, 1: 45–51

Bruch H., & Ghoshal S. (2002) *Beware the Busy Manager*. Boston: Harvard Business School Press.

Business Week (2005) Special Report: Get creative!; August 1, 2005.

Conger, J. A. & Kanungo, R. N. (1987) *Charismatic Leadership in Organizations*. Thousand Oaks: Sage.

De Bono, E. (1970) *Lateral Thinking: Creativity Step by Step*. London: Harper & Row.

Hersey, P., & Blanchard, K. H. (2000) *Management of Organizational Behavior*. New Jersey: Prentice-Hall.

Killman, R. H., Pondy, L. R., & Sleven, D. (eds) (1976) *The Management of Organization in Design, Vol 1*. New York: North Holland.

Lubatkin, M. H., Simsek, Z., Ling, Y., & Veiga, J. F. (2006). Ambidexterity and performance in small- to medium-sized firms: The pivotal role of top management team behavioral integration. *Journal of Management*, 32: 646–72.

Mason, H., & Rohner, P. (2002) *The Venture Imperative. Boston:* Harvard Business School Press.

Meister, J.C. (1998) *Corporate Universities: Building a World-Class Workforce*, 2nd edn. London: McGraw-Hill.

Moore, J. F. (1996) *The Death of Competition: Leadership & Strategy in the Age of Business Ecosystems*. New York: Harper Business.

Peterson, R. S., Smith, D. B., Martorana, P. V., & Owens, P. D. (2003) The impact of chief executive officer personality on top management team dynamics: One mechanism by which leadership affects organizational performance. *Journal of Applied Psychology*, 88(5): 795–808.

Prahalad, C. K., & Krishnan, M. S. (2008) *The New Age of Innovation: Driving Co-created Value through Global Networks*. London: McGraw Hill.

Porter, M.E. (1980) *Competitive Strategy*. New York: Free Press.

Smith, W. K., & Tushman, M. L. (2005). Managing strategic contradictions: A top management model for managing innovation streams. *Organization Science*, 16: 522–36.

Index

Printed and bound by CPI Group (UK) Ltd, Croydon, CR0 4YY